Madame Melville
and
The General from America

D1526992

By the same author

Plays

Early Plays Vol. 1:
The Killing of Yablonski, Conjuring an Event,
Jungle Coup, Scooping

Early Plays Vol. 2:
Bal, The Return of Pinocchio, The Vienna Notes

Early Plays Vol. 3:
An American Comedy, Jitterbugging: Scenes of Sex in a New
Society (after Schnitzler), Rip Van Winkle or "The Works"
Roots in Water
Between East and West
Principia Scriptoriae
Left
Some Americans Abroad
Two Shakespearean Actors
Columbus and the Discovery of Japan
Life Sentences
Misha's Party (with Alexander Gelman)
New England
The General from America
Kenneth's First Play (with Colin Chambers)
Goodnight Children Everywhere
Madame Melville

Adaptations

Don Juan by Moliere
Il Campiello by Goldoni
The Wedding by Brecht

Jungle of Cities by Brecht
The Suicide by Erdman
The Marriage of Figaro by Beaumarchais
Accidental Death of an Anarchist by Dario Fo
Three Sisters by Chekhov
The Father by Strindberg
The Wood Demon by Chekhov
Miss Julie by Strindberg
The Seagull by Chekhov

Musicals

James Joyce's The Dead (book and co-lyricist)
Chess (book)

Screenplays

Ethan Frome
End of a Sentence

Radio Plays (for BBC)

Languages Spoken Here
Eating Words
Advice to Eastern Europe
The American Wife

Nonfiction

Making Plays: The Writer-Director Relationship in the
Theatre Today (with David Jones, edited by Colin Chambers)

Madame Melville
and
The General from America

RICHARD NELSON

Grove Press
New York

Published simultaneously in Canada
Printed in the United States of America

FIRST EDITION

Library of Congress Cataloging-in-Publication Data

Nelson, Richard, 1950–
    Madame Melville ; and, The general from America / by Richard Nelson.—1st ed.
      p. cm.
    ISBN 0-8021-3844-6
    1. Arnold, Benedict, 1741–1801—Drama. 2. Teacher-student relationships—Drama.
3. Paris (France)—Drama. 4. Women teachers—Drama. 5. Teenage boys—Drama.
6. Seduction—Drama. 7. Generals—Drama. I. Title: Madame Melville ; and, The general from America. II. Nelson, Richard, 1950– General from America. III. Title:
General from America. IV. Title.
    PS3564.E4747 M33 2001
    812'.54—dc21   2001040868

Grove Press
841 Broadway
New York, NY 10003

01 02 03 04 10 9 8 7 6 5 4 3 2 1

CONTENTS

MADAME MELVILLE

For Michael Nelson

"One can take all possible liberties of
line, form, proportions, colors
to make feeling intelligible
and clearly visible."
—Pierre Bonnard

Madame Melville was first produced at the Vaudeville Theatre, London, on October 18, 2000, produced by Ostar Enterprises, Gregory Mosher, Freddy DeMann, Andrew Fell, Adam Kenwright, and Michael Fuchs, with the following cast:

CARL   Macaulay Culkin

CLAUDIE   Irène Jacob

RUTH   Madeleine Potter

FATHER   Aidan Watts

Director   Richard Nelson
Set Designer   Thomas Lynch
Costume Designer   Fotini Dimou
Lighting Designer   Peter Mumford
Sound Designer   Scott Myers
Associate Director   Colin Chambers
Stage Management   Michael Townsend, Andrew Ralph, Vicki Warwick

Madame Melville was subsequently presented at the Promenade Theatre, New York, on May 3, 2001, produced by Ostar Enterprises, Gregory Mosher, Julian Schlossberg, and Ben Sprecher, in association with Sunny Evertt, Ted Tulchin, Darren Bagert, and Aaron Levy, with the following cast:

CARL   Macaulay Culkin

CLAUDIE   Joely Richardson

RUTH   Robin Weigert

FATHER   Steve Todar

Director   Richard Nelson
Set Designer   Thomas Lynch
Costume Designer   Susan Hilferty
Lighting Designer   Jennifer Tipton
Sound Designer   Scott Myers
Stage Management   Matthew Silver, Dan da Silva

Characters

CARL

CLAUDIE

RUTH

FATHER

SETTING

An apartment in Paris in 1966

An apartment. Paris. 1966. Exit to the hallway and front door, another to kitchen, a third to bathroom and bedroom. Bookcases, record player, and record albums, etc.

CARL, a fifteen-year-old American, reads to the audience from a small paperback:

CARL

> "because she hath
> A lovely boy, stolen from an Indian king . . .
> And she perforce withholds the loved boy,
> Crowns him with flowers and makes him all her joy."

(*He closes the book and puts it back in the bookcase.*) I think I was nearly thirty before I saw an actual stage production of *A Midsummer Night's Dream.* (*The book replaced, he turns back to the audience.*) The young man speaking to you is the same age I was in 1966. When I last visited this room. Which long ago ceased to exist. Today I am nearing fifty myself, with wife and children—one nearly fifteen himself—but I could not find it in my imagination to see myself, to place the man I am today here. In this room. For when I think of her, or when I speak of her, in the middle of a thought, in the middle of a dream, I am forever—a boy of fifteen. With a voice like this boy's—honest, simple, thoughtful, and not yet—uncertain. The uncertainty—that happened here. (*He looks over the room one more time, then:*) Recently I came across an interesting discussion of that word by a professor in New Jersey. "Uncertainty," he said, "is the tentativeness created from seeing many things from many points of view."

7

Short pause.

Uncertainty then is one of the first essential steps toward becoming a writer.

Beat.

The simple facts first. (*He smiles at the irony of this.*) What a devious, insidious phrase. (*Then, continuing:*) Anyway—we arrived in Paris in the winter, 1966.

Beat.

1966. When you felt the world about to burst its seams. They hadn't snapped yet, but you couldn't help but feel— any time.

Beat.

1966. My father, a businessman, had already been here six months, and when his project expanded we were brought over as well—my mother and me. My brother was at Cornell, smoking pot, he later confessed. And I was enrolled in the American School, where I was taught literature by Mme. Melville. I wasn't a very good student and hated Paris, which seemed—with its streets, its monuments and its people—all created to make me feel stupid. I had few friends and with those I tagged along on Fridays to the Bus Palladium, where—and this was supposed to excite me—we could dance like in America.

Beat.

It was at the Bus Palladium that I first heard the name the Rolling Stones—and where I first watched a young bearded American enthrall a crowd of French girls as he burned what I learned through a series of breathless whispers was his draft card. Though when I saw this same young man burn it again another night, one had to wonder.

Beat.

Then, one day, out of the blue, Mme. Melville, who had hardly seemed to notice me in her class, asked—if I'd care to join her and the small group of students who met twice a week to see and discuss the very latest films. (*He closes his eyes and recites.*) *Masculine Feminine. Jules and Jim. Hiroshima, Mon Amour. Blow-Up. King of Hearts.* (*Opens his eyes*) It's where I saw my first naked women—my first *moving* naked women—in these films.

Beat.

We'd all meet at her apartment. (*Gestures "here"*) I'd return there as well for chocolates or cocoa or tea. She'd always put music on.

He moves the record-player arm and a piece by Bach begins to play.

Music I was careful not to admit not knowing. Music so beautiful . . . Music I had to ask, I had to wonder, why did I not know such music? There was never any music in my house—only what my brother played on his record player. So I knew only that. I had never in my life been to a concert—of such music. The other students in the film group talked about how they liked so-and-so's version of this or that better than someone else's version, and I tried to agree. Tried to smile knowingly, but not too aggressively, as I did not wish to be actually brought into the conversation. (*Turns and looks*) And there were books— books upon books, bookcases filled with books. Both here and in her bedroom. In Mme. Melville's bedroom. (*Gestures*) Through there.

9

Beat.

I looked at all these books, and while others around me discussed what was in them—they had read them!—I—I touched them.

Short pause. The Bach continues to play.

And so it was on one Friday evening, in early summer, with school nearly over for the year, that we watched a film about American surfboarders traveling the world looking for big waves, and we strolled as a pack back through the ghost-lit Paris streets, past the gates of the Sorbonne, and up the wiry toy elevator until we were here, where I, while in the toilet, heard first the doorbell, then voices, and the group's loud and many good-byes.

From the hallway door, we hear these "good-byes" off.

And found myself suddenly in the middle of her living room, alone. So I picked up my jacket to go . . .

CLAUDIE MELVILLE, *French, in her thirties and very attractive, enters from the hallway. Carl pretends to be finishing zipping up his fly. Classical music plays.*

CLAUDIE (*Surprised*)   You're still here, Carl? You're not leaving with—?

CARL (*Over this*)   Where are the others? I was—(*Gestures toward the toilet*)

CLAUDIE   That was Sophie's mother. She was early. Were you getting a ride with—?

CARL   They live on the other side—

CLAUDIE (*Over some of this*) That's right. You're the one who takes the Metro. You live in the other direction. Whereabouts do you—?

CARL Sixteenth—

Throughout this Claudie has appeared very distracted.

CLAUDIE (*Not listening*) Have some chocolates. No one ate any chocolates.

CARL I did.

CLAUDIE Then have some more.

She takes a chocolate. Picks up a pile of mail, looks through it, sighs. Carl watches her for a moment, then:

CARL I should go.

She turns and looks at him.

CLAUDIE Sophie's mother came too early.

CARL (*Explaining*) The Metro closes in—

CLAUDIE Not yet. You've got a little bit of time. (*Continues to look through her mail, then looks up*) Unless there's someplace you have to . . .

CARL No.

CLAUDIE (*Finishing with her mail*) Or I can drive you home. (*She sets the mail down, looks at him and smiles.*) And take off that tie. I detest ties on boys. And push back your hair. Straight back.

He does.

That's better. (*She goes to him and holds his hair back*) I'm going to have a wine. What about you? Coca-Cola? Orangina? Mineral water? (*She heads for the kitchen.*)

CARL I'll have wine too.

She turns back to look at him; he pretends to look at her books.

CLAUDIE If there's anything that interests you . . .

He looks up, confused.

Take what you want.

Still confused.

Borrow a book.

He understands. She goes to the albums and pulls out one and hands it to Carl as she heads for the kitchen.

CLAUDIE Put that on, will you please, Carl?

She goes; the music continues.

(*From the kitchen*) Did you see Lucy's skirt? Did you notice that? Of course you noticed that. You're a boy! The school rule says across the top of the knee. She must have rolled it up during the film. Is that what she did? You were sitting next to her.

CARL (*Calls to the kitchen*) No. No, I wasn't. That was Robert.

CLAUDIE (*Entering with a glass of wine and a glass of Orangina*) Robert? Then perhaps *he* rolled it up.

CARL I don't think—

CLAUDIE Here (*the Orangina*). I thought William was Lucy's boyfriend. That's not what I was feeling tonight. What happened to the (*record*)—

CARL I'm sorry . . .

As he puts on the new album:

CLAUDIE Skirts are going way, way up. That's what everyone's saying. Inches. Out of sight! As you Americans say. (*She smiles at him.*) Soon, you men will say—why bother. Right?

Before he can respond, the music comes on: Stephane Grappelli.

  Sh—sh. (*She sits on the sofa, kicks off her shoes, closes her eyes.*)

Long pause.

Claudie is lost in thought as she sips her wine and gently sways to the jazz.

Carl watches her closely, then after a while takes out a new, unopened packet of cigarettes. He hesitates, then:

CARL Cigarette?

She opens her eyes and looks at him.

CLAUDIE (*With a half smile*) I didn't know you—

CARL I do. (*He doesn't.*)

She hesitates, then leans over him, puts her hand on his thigh for balance and takes a cigarette. She lets him light it. The music continues. She looks at his face, then brushes back his hair again.

CARL It doesn't stay.

CLAUDIE It will. We need to train it, so that after a while it won't dare not to. (*Smiles, smokes*) What did you think of the film tonight?

CARL Not very much.

CLAUDIE Because it was American?

13

CARL   Why would that matter?

She shrugs.

I just got bored. A film about guys surfing . . .

CLAUDIE   It's very popular with the kids.

CARL   I'm not a kid.

CLAUDIE   No.

Beat.

I liked seeing the boys in their bathing suits. That kept me interested. It kept the girls interested. Sophie says she's going to go back and see it again. And bring her mother. (*Laughs lightly*)

CARL (*Still serious*)   I liked the films we've been seeing. The more serious ones.

CLAUDIE   This was serious.

CARL   A bunch of rather thick guys going surfing.

CLAUDIE   About a bunch of "guys" searching, Carl. On a quest—for that one perfect wave. It was mythological. Homeric. But not for you. Fair enough. You liked the French films about sex.

CARL   They're not about—

CLAUDIE   How well are you doing in your other classes, Carl? I haven't heard about any problems, still—

CARL   I'm fine.

CLAUDIE   You're a bright boy.

CARL   Thank you.

14

CLAUDIE   You could do better in my class.

Beat.

You could speak more.

CARL   I pay attention.

CLAUDIE   That's not what I said—I said you could assert
yourself more. We'd all like to know what you're thinking.
(*Changing the subject*) I think Lucy's getting set to dump
William. And I think it was for Robert that she was raising
her skirt. What do you think?

CARL (*After a beat*)   I think it doesn't have to be *for* anyone.
That's not how everything always is.

CLAUDIE   I think you're wrong there. I think I'm right.

They listen to the music.

She sips, takes a puff, then, as if suddenly realizing:

Did you stay in the toilet until the others had left? Is that
what you were doing?

CARL   I didn't hear—

CLAUDIE   You didn't hear the bell? You didn't hear Sophie's
very loud mother?

CARL (*Over this, too emphatic*)   No. No!

CLAUDIE   You didn't know everyone was leaving?

CARL   No! (*He stands.*) I should go.

CLAUDIE   You weren't trying—on purpose—to stay behind? I
think you were, Carl. And—I think there is nothing
remotely wrong with that. (*He is frozen in place.*) But then
again, maybe you didn't know why you were staying back. I

think men often don't know what makes them do the things they do. I think that is why women find men so—dangerous.

Beat.

And so—terrible. (*She is lost in her thoughts for an instant, then:*) And of course men find women dangerous for totally different reasons. Isn't that true? (*Smiles, sort of teasing, sort of flirting*) We were talking about just this in class this week, weren't we? Drink your Orangina. (*He takes the glass and drinks; she continues without a beat.*) The books women have written about men—such as they are, and those by men about women. How different they are. It wasn't exactly on the curriculum; I snuck it in. Very bold of me, wasn't it? I looked to you two or three times in the discussion to join us. To tell us what you know about what men think about women. You must know a lot.

Beat.

Don't you?

He sits back down and drinks his Orangina. As she continues, he fiddles with the magazines, etc., on the coffee table.

Next time—participate. Still I'm so happy you're in my class. So nice to see your attentive face there. Though I keep wanting to push that hair back.

She smiles. He looks up and half smiles. He has his hand on a magazine.

Look at that. Have you seen it?

CARL (*Looking at the magazine*)   No.

CLAUDIE   High school kids published that. From Pavini High School—Do you know where—?

CARL No.

CLAUDIE *La Zanzara*. Do you know what it means?

CARL The mosquito.

CLAUDIE Very good. Nice name for a student—

CARL I don't think so.

CLAUDIE You haven't read—It's been in the news. Been all sorts of arguments—They discuss divorce, birth control, sexual education. High school students. Like you. The world is changing fast. If you wish to borrow that.

CARL I don't.

Short pause. He puts the magazine down, picks up a book.

CLAUDIE That's right. It's not exactly your kind of thing, is it?

CARL What do you mean?

CLAUDIE I mean—you wish to be a writer yourself, don't you?

Beat.

A poet, isn't it?

No response.

(*As if responding to his question*) Who told me? Did Lucy tell me? (*She smiles.*) I think it was your father who told me.

CARL I didn't know you'd ever met my father.

CLAUDIE Before you enrolled. He came to school to discuss you before he'd enroll you. We had a nice talk.

CARL He's never said he met you.

CLAUDIE Why would he? Do you talk about me at home?

Beat.

And he might not even remember me. He saw so many teachers that day. But I remember very well him saying his son wanted to be a poet. And then he laughed. I didn't like your father.

Beat.

I said to him that the world needed all the poets it can get. How come you haven't shown me any of your poems? What are they about?

Beat.

Lucy?

Beat.

You *were* sitting next to her, Carl. You were sitting on her left. And I watched you maneuver to make sure you did, too.

CARL Like I "maneuvered" to stay behind here?

Pause.

CLAUDIE I'll tell you a funny story I heard on the radio. Hand me another of those (*cigarettes*). And look through (*record albums*)—if there's something you want to (*hear*) . . .

She lights her cigarette and puts her feet up on Carl's chair, against his leg.

This man's a novelist. He's written maybe three or four published novels. One day he's riding the Metro and he sees the man next to him reading one of his books. He checks out what page he's on. Eighty-three. Well, he knows for sure there is a very funny incident on page eighty-nine. So he waits. He goes past his stop and waits. Then while the man is on page eighty-nine—the author watches him laugh out loud.

Beat.

Then and there the writer decided to give up novels and write plays. (*Laughs*) He needed an audience! So don't be a poet, Carl—be a playwright! (*Finishes her wine*) I think we all need audiences, don't you? I was thinking, getting our drinks—by the way there's more Orangina if—

CARL   I drink wine.

Beat.

She gets up and heads for the kitchen.

CLAUDIE   I was thinking when I was in the kitchen, how nice—(*She is off and continues, off.*)—it is that you did stay back tonight. I really didn't feel like sitting here alone. (*She returns with a bottle of wine and a glass for Carl. For a moment as she sits she is lost in her thoughts, then:*) Sophie's mother came about a half an hour early. Do you know Sophie very well? The conferences I have had about Sophie—I shouldn't be telling you this. (*She pours the wine.*) She's a real bitch. Not like your Lucy. Cheers. Or what do you say in America?

CARL   I don't know.

She sits back down on the sofa and draws her feet up under her. Carl takes his wine. She sips hers, looks around, somewhat distracted, then, noticing the magazine again:

CLAUDIE   So that high school magazine doesn't interest you.

Pause. The music is over. There is a silence in the room. Claudie doesn't know what to say, then:

CLAUDIE Be a playwright! (*Toasts him, then finally:*) Now you say something.

CARL (*After a beat*) I did stay back on purpose. I waited in the toilet until I heard they were gone.

Puffs her cigarette, then:

CLAUDIE Don't be too honest, it's not attractive.

He turns away, hurt.

But on the other hand, don't always just accept what a woman says. She's not always saying everything she means and that, I think it's fair to say, is an understatement. So— one can, a man can laugh at what she says. Put her in her place. No woman wants to be boss all of the time.

Beat.

It's your conversation now. Lead away. (*She waits, watches him, then:*)

CARL Are you a Catholic?

CLAUDIE (*Not what she expected*) Why do you—?

CARL The cross (*around her neck*). And I saw on the toilet wall—

CLAUDIE Yes, I'm a Catholic.

CARL Do you go to Mass?

CLAUDIE I have.

CARL Could I go with you sometime?

CLAUDIE You want to become a Catholic?

CARL I want to go to a mass.

Beat.

There's a writer I like. A poet. I've been reading about him. He became a Catholic. So I'm interested in—

CLAUDIE Not all good poets become Catholics.

CARL I know—

CLAUDIE Not all poets who become Catholic are good—

CARL I know that, Mme. Melville!

It is the first time he has used her name this evening. The formality stops the conversation and changes its tone.

CLAUDIE (*Quietly*) You don't go to any church?

CARL My parents do. I don't.

CLAUDIE Does that trouble them?

No response.

Anything else? It is still your conversation.

Beat.

And yes, I will take you to Mass if you wish. But let me give you a little advice. When you are alone with a girl, don't, right off, start talking about religion. (*She smiles.*)

CARL Am I with a girl now?

She stops smiling.

CLAUDIE No. No, you're not. (*Claudie leans over and looks through the albums. Without looking at him*) Did you like the Grappelli?

No response.

We've just been listening to Stephane Grappelli.

CARL   I don't know what I like yet.

She continues to look.

How could I? And yes, I would very much like to borrow some books. That's why, to tell the truth—I stayed behind tonight. To see if I could—

CLAUDIE (*Without looking at him*)   Please. Look.

CARL   And the reason I hardly speak in school or here—or at the films—is because I don't have anything that's worth saying.

CLAUDIE   I doubt if you believe that.

CARL   It's true. If you could hear some of my thoughts. Some of the things I've almost said? (*He tries to laugh.*) I laugh at myself all the time. Better me than you.

CLAUDIE   I wouldn't laugh—

CARL   I'll tell you something that's true. At the beginning of the term, when the class books were handed out? I lined them up in my room at home. And measured their thickness with my hands and told myself—Carl, in a few more months you'll know at least this much. (*Shows the width with his fingers*)

CLAUDIE   I'm not laughing. But speaking to you as a teacher now—

CARL   How else have you been speaking?

CLAUDIE (*Over the end of this*)   I would ask you, when you hear a new piece of music or see for the first time a great painting—not to worry how many "inches" of knowledge is that? I'm saying, Carl, that perhaps it's not something that needs to be measured.

He looks at her, then continues.

CARL In class last week you spoke about rhyme. How in English, because there aren't so many words that rhyme, when one does it's to show off—your mind, your cleverness. Whereas in French, with so many, you rhyme as the heart pumps, as you breathe, as the eyes blink.

CLAUDIE I must be a better teacher than I thought; none of you seemed to be—

CARL I don't know what you mean. It doesn't make sense to me. (*Recites*)
   "*Oui, puisque je retrouve un ami si fidèle,*
   Ma fortune va prendre une face nouvelle."
(*Explains*) The opening of *Andromaque*.

CLAUDIE Yes. (*She smiles.*)

CARL I learned it so I could speak as one breathes, as one's eyes open and shut. (*Continues*)
   "*Et déjà son courroux semble s'être adouci*
   Depuis qu'elle a pris soin de nous rejoindre ici."

CLAUDIE Good for you, Carl. You should recite for the class—

CARL No. You talked about reading Proust? I've never read a word he's written.

CLAUDIE You're young. You will.

CARL You said, Mme. Melville, that to read Proust you must prepare as though for your honeymoon, when one knows that over a period of days two lifetimes will be forever entwined, joined together, where passion spent only sows more passion and more nights together, and mornings, and long, gray afternoons.

Beat.

What does that mean? I really want to know what that means. Every day I notice things, Mme. Melville. Every day I hear myself speak, think—I want to know. I write down notes, I imagine asking you.

Beat.

CLAUDIE Ask me.

CARL *The Magic Flute.* What's it about? What does it sound like?

CLAUDIE That's easy, I have the album here.

Then, before she can look:

CARL William Faulkner.

CLAUDIE Yes?

CARL I bought a book. I can't figure it—

CLAUDIE Which one?

CARL I don't know how to pronounce it. *Absalom—(He mispronounces it.)*

CLAUDIE Let me loan you another. That's the hardest, I think.

CARL *(On to the next)* The painting in your hallway. The woman in the bathtub.

CLAUDIE The print.

CARL *(Over this)* Whose is it?

CLAUDIE (*Going to the bookcase*) Pierre Bonnard. I have a book.

She finds the book.

CARL You said in class one day that you'd been an actress—

CLAUDIE For only a year, years a—

CARL And singer. (*She brings the book back and sets it down.*) And just before Easter you sang a song. What was that song?

CLAUDIE It was just before Lent. And we'd had wine in the faculty lunchroom—

CARL What is the song, Claudie?

His saying her first name stops her.

I'm sorry I—

CLAUDIE No. Don't be sorry. I like my name.

Claudie hesitates, then quietly sings a short bit of an Edith Piaf song. She suddenly stops, turns and rubs Carl's hair.

I think the Opera House will be doing *The Magic Flute*. Let me take you.

CARL (*On to another question*) In the toilet—on the walls. You did that? It's a collage?

CLAUDIE Yes, I suppose so. It's—

CARL From books. Postcards. Magazines. You did that?

CLAUDIE I did.

CARL Of naked men and women.

CLAUDIE Mostly.

CARL And words. You also cut out of—

CLAUDIE It's supposed to be—fun. Funny. Something to look at in the toilet. Is that what kept you in there? The naked women—?

CARL It's not important, then.

CLAUDIE No, it—

CARL I'm not missing something?

CLAUDIE It is not—It's meaningless, Carl. It was done for— to be funny.

CARL (*Having picked up the art book*) Pierre Bonnard. Is he important?

CLAUDIE He is to me.

CARL Why?

Beat.

You don't know why?

CLAUDIE I know why.

He looks at her.

Because there was a man—this was years and years ago— and he took me to a gallery. We first had lunch, then we passed the gallery where there was an exhibition of Bonnard. He took me in; we went from painting to painting. I remember each painting. I remember him holding with his hand my arm, and steering me from painting to painting, and asking me—what do I think? What does it make me feel? What do I see? (*She turns a few pages in the book.*) We went back out into the bright sunlight. It was June. Like now. We went to his apartment. And we made love. We then lived together for nearly three years.

26

They look at the book.

CARL Is this the book from that exhibition?

CLAUDIE No. I didn't have money then to buy art books. I bought this later.

They turn pages, then:

CARL And if you hadn't gone with this man that day to this exhibition, you wouldn't think Bonnard important?

CLAUDIE Probably not. Certainly not in the same way.

They look at one picture.

What do you see? (*She takes his arm.*) What does it make you feel?

He looks at her, then back at the picture.

CARL A woman after a bath. A nude woman.

Beat.

She is rubbing, cleaning her thigh with a cloth? One foot on a stool—no, it's a chair. She's wearing green shoes or slippers. She's looking down.

CLAUDIE What makes you say she has taken a bath?

CARL Because the water's in the tub. She wouldn't let the water sit there and get cold. She'd get in.

She smiles.

What? Why is that funny—?

CLAUDIE Not funny. I think maybe I said almost the same thing to my teacher. We are two practical people, Carl. (*She squeezes his arm.*) And I think he smiled at me too.

CARL   Your teacher? The man who took you to—

CLAUDIE   And he stood me in front of this very painting for a long long time before we spoke. "Is she alone?" he finally asked me. "There's no one else in the picture," I answered. "Or," and he turned and looked at me, "is someone watching her?" I hadn't thought of that. "Is she aware that someone is—watching her? The painter of this picture? Monsieur Bonnard? Perhaps," he continued, looking back at the painting, "the bath has been run for *him*. Perhaps," he continued now, putting his arm around my shoulder (*Puts her arm around Carl's shoulder*), "she has left their bedroom, walked naked as we now see her, her green slippers clapping upon the hardwood floor or whispering across the carpet, her toes cracking as she passes their disheveled bed and into the hallway, and into—here. Her mission: to run *him* a bath. And so now, as she waits, she cleans herself of their lovemaking. Cleans off the 'him' that got onto her. While he, standing naked unseen in the doorway, watches."

Pause. They look at the painting. Her arm is still around him.

And then my teacher said, "It may not be what Bonnard intended, Mlle. Melville. But it's what being here with you has let me see."

Short pause.

Twenty minutes later we're in his bed making love.

They look at the picture, then she turns the page.

(*About the next painting*) With this I only see fruit in a bowl on a table. Nothing else. (*Suddenly hears something*) Sh—sh. (*Listens, then:*) I thought it might be Ruth. She lives next (*door*)—(*She gestures.*) But it's from upstairs? (*She takes his*

28

hand in hers and listens; then, in a whisper:) An old man lives up there. I think he works in a publishing office. He's heavy and he walks like—(*Mimics heavy steps*) But some days— nights—one hears—(*Mimics light steps*) Listen.

He tries to listen, but she now gently rubs his back.

A young woman, Carl? A young man? Definitely two different sets of steps. But I have never seen anyone but the gentleman on the stairs. (*Half to herself*) You hear sounds— you can imagine all sorts of things. Things people are doing. (*Suddenly back to Ruth*) Ruth's out on a—What time is it? She should be—(*Looks at Carl's watch*) Oh God, look at the time! (*Suddenly stands*) Carl, when's the last Metro?

CARL (*At the same time*)   I think I've (*missed it*)—.

CLAUDIE (*At the same time*)   You haven't missed the last Metro?

CARL   It's too late.

CLAUDIE (*Over this*)   How could we be so stupid!

CARL   I'm sorry to make you drive me.

CLAUDIE   But I can't drive you.

CARL   You offered—You said—

CLAUDIE (*Over some of this*)   When did I—? I wasn't thinking. My car's in the garage, Carl. I told you that. I told you that when we were waiting in line at the film.

CARL   That's right. You did.

Beat.

I'll walk home then. (*He looks at Claudie.*)

CLAUDIE   You can't walk to the Sixteenth, Carl.

CARL Why not?

CLAUDIE What about a taxi?

At first neither has an answer for this.

CLAUDIE I'll phone your mother; she'll have to drive over and—

CARL She doesn't drive at all in Paris.

CLAUDIE I think you told me that.

Beat.

And your father—won't be home yet?

CARL He's entertaining business friends. They could be out half the night.

Beat.

CLAUDIE What do we do? (*Then the answer about the taxi*) I don't have money for a taxi to—

CARL Neither do I.

Beat.

CLAUDIE What are we going to do?

Beat.

CARL I don't know.

Claudie rubs her head.

CLAUDIE I feel so stupid. I feel responsible—

CARL You're not responsible for me. I'm not a child.

She looks at him.

CLAUDIE   No. No, you are not. (*She smiles.*) There's the couch. You could stay here on the—It's not too comfortable. But what would your mother—?

CARL   I don't want to be any trouble.

CLAUDIE   It is my fault.

They look at each other. The entire previous "conversation" has almost been spoken in quotes.

And you would be no trouble.

CARL   I'll leave early. When the Metro—

CLAUDIE   Right after breakfast. First let me give you breakfast.

They look at each other, then:

CARL   I'll call then . . . My mother.

Claudie looks at him, shrugs: "What else can we do?" Carl goes to the phone and dials.

(*Into the phone*) Hello, Mom? I've missed the last subway. We got talking and—That's a lot of money to waste on—Mme. Melville's said I could stay on—their couch. I've said that. She says—Here, Mom, she wants to talk to you.

He holds out the phone. Claudie hadn't wanted to talk, but now has no choice.

CLAUDIE   (*Clears her throat, sets down her wineglass, then:*)   Hello? Mrs.—No. It is no bother at all. And it is all my fault. We got to talking about the film tonight and—Please.

Beat.

I don't mind, I assure you. Yes. I just don't know how I could be so stupid. Good. I will have him call the first thing. What? (*She gives Carl's mother her phone number.*) Medisee 4207. You're welcome. (*Starts to hang up, then:*) He's a very good student. You should be proud of him. Good night. (*Hangs up.*) She says it's fine. She doesn't mind.

Short pause. For a moment neither knows what to say, then:

CARL   A lot of fifteen-year-old boys stay out until God knows when. And with God knows who. At least she knows I'm with my—teacher.

Claudie nods at this thought, then suddenly hears footsteps upstairs.

CLAUDIE   Listen. The old man's got company. A girl or a boy? What do you think?

Beat.

As they listen:

Sometimes you also hear . . . noises. Let me get some sheets for the sofa.

She goes.

CARL   She thinks you have a husband.

CLAUDIE (*Off*)   What?

Returns with sheets. She looks at him.

CARL   She thinks—there's a husband—(*Gestures "here"*)

Beat.

My mother thinks—She asked the other day—if Mme. Melville's husband went to the films with us.

Beat.

I think because of the "Madame."

Claudie starts to make the bed; Carl tries to help.

CLAUDIE   The school asked me to use—

CARL   I know.

CLAUDIE   And what did you answer? About whether Mme. Melville's husband went to the films?

CARL   I said—he hasn't so far. I guess he doesn't like films.

She looks at him and smiles.

CLAUDIE   (*As they continue*)   I don't have men's pajamas . . .

CARL   I don't need—

CLAUDIE   I keep a few new toothbrushes—I'll set one out.

CARL   (*Innocently*)   Why do you keep new—(*Stops himself*)

She watches him as they finish up the bed, pillows, etc. Then, as if out of the blue, to say something:

CLAUDIE   School's almost over. What are you doing for the vacation?

CARL   My mother and I are going back to the States.

Claudie nods, lights a cigarette, offers one to Carl, who shakes his head, and they continue with the couch, etc.

CLAUDIE   (*Getting the cigarette*)   Whereabouts in the States—?

CARL   Ohio.

CLAUDIE   Where's that?

CARL   In the—

CLAUDIE Never mind.

Beat.

You looking forward to that?

No response.

I'll miss you. It's late, we should both get to bed. You want to use the bathroom first?

He hesitates, then looks toward the toilet; she stops him.

I might have something you could wear.

CARL I don't need—

CLAUDIE Let me see how—

She measures his shoulders.

CARL (*Quietly*) I'm fine in my underwear.

He looks at her, then goes off to the bathroom. Pause. Claudie finishes the last little bit of bed-making, starts to pick up the wine and glasses, then decides to pour herself another glass.
We hear water running in the bathroom sink.
She sits down on the couch, sips her drink. Her eye catches the Bonnard book; she picks it up and starts to look through it.
Toilet flushes off, and Carl returns.

CARL It's all (*yours*)—

CLAUDIE (*Over the book*) I then had to write a paper. My boyfriend who was also my teacher—who had taken me to see—he assigned a paper on art. And I wrote about Bonnard. I described this painting just as he had described it to me.

She turns to Carl, puffs on her cigarette.

I got the paperback, Carl—and it was full of red marks. Where're your critics? Where's your research? Where's your thinking? This is supposed to be an essay, not a sentimental journey! (*She smiles, bemused, shakes her head.*) "Think for yourself," he wrote, at the top.

She closes the book; Carl tries to smile.

Teachers, right? (*And she sighs.*) You are finished?

He nods.

Anything you need—?

He shakes his head.

Then—good night.

CARL Good night.

She stops and goes right up to him, hesitates, then holds out her hand for him to shake.

CLAUDIE Good night.

They shake hands and she goes off to the bathroom.
He turns off the lights; light now pours from the hallway and bathroom. In the dark, Carl takes off his pants and shirt and gets under the sheets on the sofa.
Immediately Claudie, still dressed, returns and picks up her wineglass.

(*"Explaining"*) I didn't finish my wine.

She sips. He doesn't move. In the darkness, she sniffles; it is clear that she is trying not to cry. Carl doesn't know what to do, then:

CARL Are you okay?

CLAUDIE Yes. (*She smiles.*) Yes. I am okay. (*She sighs.*) Tonight, I am so happy not to be alone. Thank you. (*She*

35

finishes her wine.) Here. Give me your hand. Give me your palm. (*She sits on the couch and he gives her his hand. She tickles the palm with her finger.*) Do you know what this means? When someone does this to your palm?

Beat.

It means they want to have sex with you. (*She tickles again.*) Like this. So if Lucy ever . . . Now you'll know. There aren't enough hours in the day to teach everything in school. (*She starts to get up, stops, and suddenly holds out her palm.*)

Want to try it?

He is frozen. She gets up, rubs his head and leaves, but immediately returns with a robe.

Try this on. I think it should fit. Stand up and try it on.

Carl hesitates getting out of bed in his underwear, but does, and stands, embarrassed, as she holds up the robe. He takes it from her and puts it on. Claudie stands back and looks.

That's better. In case you have to, now you don't have to walk around here just in your underwear.

CARL (*Softly*) Good night.

He stands and watches her.
    Claudie has gone to the records and begun looking through them. After a moment, he half sits up and watches her, then:

CLAUDIE Will, this (*music*) bother you? I don't want to keep you up.

CARL No. It won't bother me.

CLAUDIE Sometimes music helps me get to sleep.

Beat.

CARL (*Quietly*)   Me too.

She puts on an album: more jazz—perhaps Wayne Shorter or Charlie Parker.
  Claudie sits on the floor and listens. She moves to the music, closing her eyes.
  She sips from her drink as the music plays for a while. Suddenly she stands up, startling Carl.

CLAUDIE (*Standing*)   I know something you would be interested in. You weren't asleep?

He shakes his head.

  There's a book—Come on. Get up. (*She starts to pull him up.*)

CARL   Where are we—?

CLAUDIE (*Over this*)   I want to show you this book. It's in my bedroom.

CARL   What sort of—

CLAUDIE (*Over this*)   Sh—sh. (*Referring to the music*) Listen to that. I love that. Don't you love that? You are sleeping in the robe, Carl? How funny you are. You are very funny. Please, do you wish to see this book or not?

CARL   What—?

CLAUDIE   It's an art book, Carl. (*Finishes her wine*) Come on. (*She takes his arm and leads him off.*)

CARL (*Heading off*)   An art book?

They are off.

The music continues to play. Carl returns, still in his robe, now holding the "art" book—an illustrated Kama Sutra *of Vatsyayana. As the jazz continues under him, he speaks to the audience.*

This was the art book. (*Opens and reads*) "Man is divided into three classes, the hare man, the bull man and the horse man, according to the size of his lingam. Women also, according to the depth of her yoni, is either a female deer, a mare or a female elephant."

Beat.

"There are thus three equal unions between persons of corresponding dimensions, and there are six unequal unions, when the dimensions do not correspond, or nine in all as the following table shows." (*He holds up the book to show us the table. Reading again*) "Equal: Hare/Deer. Bull/Mare. Horse/Elephant. Unequal—"

Beat.

Well—you can read it for yourself. The book, I've since learned, is readily available. (*Closes the book and goes and turns off the music*) Anyway, we got to looking at this book in her bedroom and at the artwork, which she said had true historical and aesthetic interest.

Beat. Carl begins to dress. As he dresses, he continues.

We lay on her bed and looked through the book. On our stomachs. Then she said she *had* to brush her teeth and she returned naked and rolled me over onto my back and undid the cord of the robe which I had already tied in a knot by accident.

Beat.

She had a design which ran across the top of her walls—
blue and white, a pattern of shapes. I stared at that, then I
closed my eyes.

Beat.

I stopped breathing. Or that's what it felt like. I heard every
sound. Felt every pump of my heart.

Beat.

She sat upon me. She put me into her. I dared not open my
eyes. My arms I kept straight against and alongside my body.

Beat.

She moved and almost instantly it happened. When I felt it,
I wanted to let her know so she could move and get off, but
she didn't move. It's the one time I opened my eyes. And
she was smiling at me.

Beat.

She moved off.

Beat.

I heard her running a bath. She called me.

CLAUDIE (*Off, calls*) Carl!

Beat.

CARL   The bath, she said, was for me. She stood, foot on
chair, cleaning herself. It was years later before I realized
what she had been doing—what she was . . . giving to me:
that Bonnard painting.

Beat.

She smiled when I came into the bathroom. She winked. And said I was very handsome.

Beat.

She never took off her small silver cross, and it swung across her breasts as she cleaned.

Beat.

In bed I lay on my stomach and tried to sleep. She put an arm over my back, a leg over my thigh, and I'm pretty sure she fell asleep this way. Holding me this way.

Beat.

Again it was years and years before the thought occurred to me that perhaps this is what I gave her—something . . . breathing to hold on to in the night.

Beat.

I watched the dawn break through her white curtains, and still did not move until I felt the light pull, tug, of her fingertips against my bare side, and I then allowed myself to be righted again upon my back, and again she put me inside of her, and it happened all again—quickly.

Beat.

This time I opened my eyes and watched her face in the morning light. Her chin. The curve of her nose. Her mouth. But I tried not to look at any other part of her nakedness. Odd as it sounds, I felt that perhaps I shouldn't. (*He begins to "unmake" the couch.*) The first train was, I think, at around six. But I remembered that she had wanted to give me breakfast.

Beat.

But she forgot about that.

Beat.

I found a roll in the kitchen. I made coffee. I lost myself in her books and records. I tried to stay out of her way, expecting to hear at any moment, "Carl, shouldn't you be going?"

Claudie, in a robe, crosses from the bedroom to the kitchen. She smiles at Carl.

But these words were never said. She never spoke them.

Carl turns up the music and begins looking through the record albums.

Pause.

Knock on the door.

Claudie hurries to answer it.

She returns following RUTH, her neighbor—American, thirty. She is dressed in messy clothes, her hair uncombed, no makeup, etc.

CLAUDIE (*Entering*) Where's—?

RUTH He's just left.

They kiss on the cheeks.

I just left him at the corner.

CLAUDIE How did it go? You met (*Carl*)—?

RUTH Hi.

CLAUDIE (*Over this*) So what's he like?

CARL (*To Ruth*) Hello.

RUTH You must be one of Claudie's students she's always talking about.

41

CARL Is she always talking about me?

RUTH (*To Claudie*) We're going to a club tonight. He knows a lot of people in clubs. Are these yours (*cigarettes*)? You don't smoke.

CLAUDIE They're Carl's.

RUTH He sings too. And plays the guitar. (*To Carl, taking a cigarette*) You don't mind?

CLAUDIE (*Over this*) Coffee? Carl, do you want coffee?

Carl holds up his cup—he has coffee.

CLAUDIE (*Over this*) Ruth's from America—

RUTH (*Continuing, not listening*) I think Robert's the first real French man I've found interesting.

Claudie moves toward the kitchen.

I don't want coffee.

Claudie stops. Ruth gestures to Carl—for a light. He picks up matches and lights her cigarette as:

By the way (*Puff*)—we heard voices last night in here. We were coming up the stairs. It was late. Was there any . . . ? (*Then she realizes that Carl is more than a student and turns to him.*) Oh.

CLAUDIE I'll have one of those too. (*Goes to take a cigarette*)

RUTH (*Looking over Carl*) I'm sorry, I didn't catch your name.

CLAUDIE Carl.

RUTH Carl. How do you do, Carl.

CLAUDIE (*Heading for the kitchen*)   You're sure you don't want (*coffee*)—(*She is gone.*)

RUTH (*Still looking over Carl*)   I'm Ruth. I live next door.

CARL   I know.

RUTH   So you're not one of Claudie's little students.

CARL   Actually—I am.

Beat.

One of her little students.

RUTH   At the American School—

CARL   Yes. (*She stares at him.*)   I'm in the tenth grade.

Claudie returns, bowl of coffee in hand.

RUTH (*To Claudie*)   He's in the tenth grade.

CLAUDIE (*Smiles, sips, then:*)   We went to see a film last night. A group of students and me. Poor Carl here missed the last train.

Short pause, as they sip, smoke, look back at the album jackets.

RUTH   Enjoy the film?

CLAUDIE   I did.

CARL   It was about surfing—

RUTH (*Over this*)   So you missed the last Metro. Poor boy.

CLAUDIE   And so he had to stay here with me. I fixed up the sofa for him. Didn't I?

Short pause. Ruth watches as Claudie looks at Carl.

CLAUDIE   Don't be embarrassed.

CARL I'm not embarrassed.

CLAUDIE Ruth understands. Don't you?

RUTH Sure.

CLAUDIE (*Suddenly to Ruth*) So tell me—what's he like?

RUTH He says I should get a bigger bed. (*Then getting "into" herself and her problems*) This from a man who says he normally sleeps on the floor—or on one of those thinny thin mattresses from the Orient? What are they called? He gets into my bed—but he is a big guy. How tall do you think Robert is?

CLAUDIE I only saw him the one—

RUTH We didn't wake you? I mean—he did play me two of his songs at something like four in the morning. I'm saying—Robert, sh—sh, sing in the morning. He says— (*French accent*) "I sing when I feel like singing."

Beat.

I've never seen a naked man strum a guitar before—you know: bouncing. It's an unnatural sight. He's got a cousin who has offered him a job. (*More random memories*) And an uncle who's somehow in the government. They don't speak. He's been to America twice. Once to Florida with his parents when he was a boy. Then once to Manhattan where he bummed around for about three weeks, living off people he just met, sleeping—wherever. Once he slept under someone's sink that had a drip. In the middle of the night, he said, they turned on a light and there he was trying to fix the drip. He's very handy. You know my record player that's been broken for weeks? He almost got it to work. That's what he said—he almost fixed it. (*She seems lost in a thought for*

44

a moment, then, changing gears, to Claudie about Carl) He's really young. (*To Carl*) Where in America are you from?

CARL Ohio.

RUTH Ohio. Never been there. I've been to Orlando, Florida. I've been to pretty much all of the East Coast states except for Maine and, I think, Rhode Island. I don't think I've been there. I'm from Montclair, New Jersey, do you know it? And New Hampshire. I haven't been there.

CARL No. I don't know it.

RUTH I tell people here that I'm from New York—same thing. But since you're an American—

CLAUDIE Ruth's been taking classes at the Sorbonne, Carl.

RUTH Among other things. But not officially. But maybe that'll happen. I'm—I just sort of follow the crowds in and sit and listen to—whatever they happen to be teaching that day. You wouldn't believe some of the courses I've been sitting in on—they're all over the map. It's how I met Robert—I was on my way to one of these classes and he was playing his guitar and singing on the Rue des Ecoles. Right around the corner from—(*Gestures*)

The phone rings. Claudie goes to answer it.

CLAUDIE (*Into phone*) Hello? Oh yes. He is. Just a minute. (*Covers phone*) Carl. It is your father. He has to come into town this morning. He can pick you up.

Holds out phone. Carl hesitates.

CARL I can take the train, he doesn't have to—

CLAUDIE Carl.

Continues to hold out the phone to him. Then as he takes it, she half whispers to him:

45

I was thinking of going to Le Louvre today. Is that something you'd like to do with me?

He looks at her.

(*Nods to the phone*) I don't know if it is all right with . . .

CARL (*Into phone*)   Dad? What? Yes, she told me. Actually— Mme. Melville—

Ruth looks at Claudie and smiles as she mouths: "Madame Melville."

—is taking a group of students to Le Louvre this—(*Turns to her*)—afternoon?

She nods.

She asked if I—It's fine, Dad. I'll take the train. Dad, she— Yes, he's coming too! Good-bye. Bye! (*He hangs up. Short pause*)

CLAUDIE   I hope I didn't create a problem, Carl.

He shakes his head.

Le Louvre is one of the most important museums in the world.

CARL   He knows that. It's fine. I can go.

CLAUDIE   Good.

RUTH (*Who has been paying close attention*)   Who's the "he" he was referring—

CLAUDIE   My husband. Carl's parents are convinced for some reason that I have a husband. I learned this last night, when they allowed Carl to stay . . .

Beat.

I suppose the "Madame." Which I use only for school.

No one knows what to say for a moment, then:

CARL He doesn't go to museums himself. They—scare him I think. My father. He doesn't like a lot of things. He doesn't like anything he doesn't understand.

Short pause.

RUTH So you two are going to Le Louvre today. With a group like you—?

CLAUDIE No. Just the two of us.

Beat.

RUTH I'd come too, but . . .

CLAUDIE But what?

RUTH But you don't want me, do you?

CLAUDIE (*Smiling*) No.

RUTH And—what's the time? (*She takes Carl's wrist and looks.*) Jesus, I have a lesson in a minute.

CARL (*To Claudie*) Lesson?

RUTH Maybe I should have some coffee, if it's no—

CLAUDIE (*On her way to the kitchen*) I'm getting it.

She is gone. Ruth sighs.

RUTH (*Looking at herself*) These are the clothes I—I almost said that I slept in—but that isn't true. (*Smiles*) That I wore last night. Just threw them on to go out for breakfast.

Claudie returns with coffee.

(*To Claudie*) I paid for breakfast by the way. My ex-husband would never have let me do that. He'd have broken my arm if I tried to do—

CLAUDIE (*To Carl*) Ruth was married back in—

RUTH Montclair.

CLAUDIE How old is Robert? He looked like he could be—

RUTH Twenty-five? Twenty-eight? Nineteen? I don't know. (*To Carl*) He's not in the third grade so you wouldn't know him.

Claudie smiles at the joke, Carl doesn't.

(*To Claudie*) Since you brought him up—

CLAUDIE Who? Robert or your ex—?

RUTH (*Over this*) What do I say about my ex-husband all the time?

CLAUDIE I don't know. So you're talking about your ex—?

RUTH About both of them. (*Turns to Carl*) Carl, when we were in school, my ex and me—he was on the track team. And he wore those cute shorts that were really shiny, like fake-silky? You know what I—

CARL They still do.

RUTH He knows them. If it weren't for those shorts!

Sits back, sips her coffee, others wait, then:

(*To Claudie*) I've told you this?

Claudie nods.

(*Referring to Carl*) Will he mind if I—?

CLAUDIE No. He won't.

RUTH (*To both of them*) I'm maybe eighteen and I accidentally touch those shorts with my hand. We're talking. Then we're—kissing and I touch.

Beat.

I lost my virginity against those shorts. I lost about eight years of my life because of those shorts. But the point I'm getting to, Claudie, is guess what kind of underwear Robert's wearing?

CLAUDIE Fake-silky?

RUTH I didn't believe it. (*To Carl*) You don't wear fake—?

CLAUDIE (*Answering for him*) No. No, he doesn't.

RUTH Oh. Anyway—so why did I bring this up?

No response. She can't remember, but continues.

So they're silky, but they are also not too clean, I noticed. You don't think he has any—disease or anything? They really weren't clean. (*Lost in thought for a moment, then:*) Anyway. Thanks for the coffee. (*She gets up, takes Carl's wrist again and looks at his watch.*) They're probably waiting outside my door.

CLAUDIE (*To Carl*) Ruth teaches violin.

RUTH (*Kissing Claudie*) Have a nice time at Le Louvre. (*To Carl*) Nice to meet you. (*Whispers to Claudie*) He's so sweet. (*She goes. Short pause*)

CLAUDIE That's my neighbor, Ruth.

Beat.

She's American. (*She rubs his shoulders as he continues to look through albums.*) Like you.

She hugs him from behind. From off (Ruth's apartment), the sound of a child's violin lesson; start and stop as he/she plays the waltz "Over the Waves."

She's also a very fine player herself. (*Leans over him and points to the albums*) Keep turning. A few more. There. Take that one out.

He takes out an album.

That's her. (*Points to a photo*) That's her all-girl quartet. It's the only album they've made so far. But they're great.

He looks at the album. Child's lesson continues off.

CARL   She didn't act like a . . .

CLAUDIE   Like a what?

CARL   I don't know. I've never met a musician before.

CLAUDIE   They're not all like—

CARL   I didn't think—

CLAUDIE   But they also don't walk around in black suits and ties and—

CARL   I know that.

CLAUDIE   Good. I should get dressed. (*She doesn't get up; she reaches and holds his hair off his face, rubs his head.*) Am I hurting you?

Beat.

I don't wish to hurt you.

She presses her face against the top of his head, sighs, then stands and goes to get dressed.

Pause. The music lesson continues. Also, slowly, the sounds of the outside begin to be heard—cars, life, street noise.

Carl speaks to the audience.

CARL That day we walked the halls and galleries of Le Louvre for six hours, occasionally resting on a bench, but always in sight of paintings to look at. The greatest paintings, she would say, that the hand of man had ever created.

Beat.

The music lesson begins to fade. Over the course of the speech, outside noise is replaced with echoing inside-the-museum noise—coughs echoing, whispers echoing, footsteps echoing.
  Then they are replaced again by the sounds of outside, along the Seine: traffic, boats, birds, children, etc.

She had walked these halls many many times before—she had favorites over which she enthused, demanding my enthusiasm. She had loves and she had hates, and she had confusions.

Beat.

She spoke with two paintings as if they were old friends— or to the people portrayed. I didn't know. She stopped to let me hear the echoing voices, and steps.

He listens.

Claudie appears in the bedroom doorway, finishing getting dressed.

CLAUDIE Never close your ears, Carl. The greatest mistake people make looking at art is to close their other senses.

But paintings live in sound. They live among these
footfalls, that child's cry. That man's cough. Those
sweethearts' whispers.

Beat.

CARL (*Continuing to the audience*)   She took me to a room she
said she hadn't visited since she was sixteen. It's known, she
said, as a great place where boys can pick up girls. Along
one wall was an Ingres, his huge portrait called "Odalisque."
A young naked woman has her back to us; she is turning,
lying, looking sensually at us. Her skin the color—and the
taste, she insisted—of honey.

Beat.

Girls came here, she explained—

CLAUDIE (*In the doorway, putting on her shoes*)—because after the
boys looked at this Ingres, every girl's ass looks inviting.
(*Claudie disappears back into her bedroom.*)

CARL   Two teenage girls sat on a side bench, hands folded in
their laps, giggling. When I turned to look at them, they
stopped and stared down. I felt Mme. Melville stick her
finger in my back pocket and pull me away—jealously, I
think. (*He smiles.*) Then as we moved, I felt her finger
stroke back and forth across my butt, inside my pocket.

Beat.

Not every painting or sculpture in Le Louvre is of a nude.
But nearly every one, or perhaps every one, is—of a body.
Mme. Melville's words.

Beat.

You take away the body, its muscles, its flesh, its sex—

CLAUDIE (*Coming out of the bedroom*)—and you empty this building. (*Fixing her stockings, brushing her hair, etc., as she prepares to go out*) Carl, a man is not only his sex . . .

CARL She said this as we stared at a painting of a very healthy-looking saint with arrows sticking through his muscular torso—

CLAUDIE (*Continuing*) But a man's sex is what makes him a man.

Beat.

CARL I said to her: "No one ever put it that way in Ohio."

As Claudie continues to get ready behind him:

One painting confused me. I remember its name—I bought a postcard of it years later. "Gabrielle d'Estrée and Her Sister."

Beat.

Two young women are shown naked from the waist up— there's a sort of curtain covering below that. One— Gabrielle or her sister?—has reached over with her hand and is pinching or holding the other's naked nipple. Both look at the artist. At us. What is this about? I asked Mme. Melville and she explained—

CLAUDIE The world's a lot more interesting than we give it credit for. (*She disappears into her room.*)

CARL Outside we walked together along the Quai du Louvre. Mme. Melville stopped at a kiosk and purchased a small book of paintings from the museum. I watched her take out her money, bending a leg to hold up the purse. The late-afternoon, early summer's sun seemed to touch her and set her apart from the world. As if a sculpture. As if a work of art.

Beat.

I felt more desire than I'd ever in my life felt before.

Beat.

The book was for me. She brushed back her hair, which the wind off the Seine kept blowing across her face. "A souvenir," she explained, as she placed it into my jacket pocket. The expression on my face, I think, stopped her, stopped her smiling. And then for the first time, though we had been together all day, all night, in her apartment, in her bed, I reached and I touched her. I touched her arm, and then held it. And I would have kissed her—until then I had never kissed a girl—but I would have kissed her had she not suddenly run off.

Short pause.

She ran to a man I recognized as Monsieur Darc, my mathematics teacher at school. With him was his young daughter, holding a balloon. They kissed each other on the cheeks. They spoke. She seemed to talk very sternly at him. They did not kiss good-bye.

Beat.

Walking home she asked if I wanted to stop for coffee. Then she ordered wine. Suddenly it was like I wasn't even there. She found a pair of sunglasses in her bag and put them on. We sat there for a long time. And then we returned to her apartment.

Carl goes to the doorway and returns with Claudie as they enter from their outing to Le Louvre.
Silence. No one speaks.
Carl takes out his new book from his jacket pocket. Claudie remains distracted.

CARL (*Holding the book*) Thank you for the—

CLAUDIE Put some music on, will you?

He hesitates.

What are you looking at? What are you looking at?

CARL (*Confused at her outburst*) What kind of music do you—?

CLAUDIE I don't care! Something! (*She takes off her shoes and heads for her bedroom. As she goes, she mumbles under her breath:*) Men.

She is gone. He puts music on. Ruth has entered; she has changed, looks great—well dressed, hair fixed, etc.

RUTH I heard you come in. Is Claudie—?

He turns toward the bedroom. As Ruth heads for the bedroom:

Can you turn that down (*the music*)?

He turns it down as Claudie comes out, putting on a sweater.

RUTH (*Explaining*) I heard you come in—

CLAUDIE (*Going to Carl*) Why can't you keep that out of your face? (*A bit aggressively, she pushes back his hair.*) And I can't hear that.

He turns the music up.

RUTH How was Le—?

CARL It was great.

CLAUDIE (*Over this*) I ran into Paul. And I'm sick and tired of running into Paul. Every day at school I have to run into Paul! There he is with a big smile on his face like nothing has happened! Buying his daughter balloons! (*Seeing Carl*) I'm sorry. Carl, you should get home.

55

CARL Why?

CLAUDIE Why? Because it is time you went home.

RUTH By the way, your mother stopped by, Carl.

CARL My mother?

RUTH She said she was your—

CLAUDIE (*Over this*) Did you give your mother my address?

CARL No. I—

CLAUDIE How did she get my address then, Carl?

RUTH She said she called the school.

CLAUDIE It's Saturday. No one's at the school.

RUTH I think she said she got the address from the headmaster at school. So I assumed she had called the—

CLAUDIE She called the headmaster at his home.

RUTH She said she was just in the neighborhood. I told her you'd probably be back . . . (*Takes Carl's wrist and looks at his watch*) soon.

Pause. No one knows what to do.

(*Noticing*) You have my album out. Have you been playing—?

CLAUDIE Not yet.

Beat.

Carl wants to hear it.

Pause. The music continues to play.

RUTH (*Standing*) I think I'm in the way—I'm sorry.

She heads off. In the hallway, Ruth bursts out crying.

CLAUDIE   Ruth? Why are you crying? (*She follows her off. Off*)
Are you all right?

*Carl sits and doesn't know what to do. Off, Claudie tries to get Ruth
to talk.*

What is it? Ruth? Tell me.

*Then mumbled talk, and Claudie leads Ruth back into the room and
immediately out into the kitchen.*

CARL   (*As they pass*)   What's—?

They are gone.

Is there anything I can do?

*Pause. Music plays. Claudie returns, crosses the room, and exits
toward the bathroom.*

What can I—?

She is gone. She returns holding a bottle of white liquid.

CLAUDIE   (*As she heads back to the kitchen*)   She has crabs. (*She
stops.*) Robert, the naked bouncing guitar player, gave her
crabs. (*She starts to go, then stops.*) You know what crabs are,
don't you?

He hesitates.

They're little—

CARL   Sure.

*She looks at him and goes. A moment later Ruth comes out, followed
by Claudie, who is holding the bottle.*

RUTH   (*Entering*)   I'll take a shower in a minute. I just got
dressed. I don't feel like taking my clothes off yet. Where
are those cigarettes?

Carl finds the cigarettes; she goes to get one.

(*To Carl*) They're really disgusting. They look just like little . . .

He moves away slightly.

You don't get them by sitting next to someone, Carl. (*She laughs to herself, then quickly turns to Claudie, wiping the tears off her face.*) How come you have a bottle of stuff for . . . (*Points to the bottle*)

Beat.

Never mind.

CARL (*To Ruth*)   Is that too loud (*the music*)?

RUTH   What?? Why are French people so unclean?!

Short pause. Claudie is hurt. Ruth realizes this. Sighs, then:

Why are men so unclean?

Ruth reaches out toward Claudie, who comes and takes her hand and sits with her. Ruth sniffles. Short pause.

CLAUDIE   I remember when I had to get that stuff (*the crabs medicine*). You have to get a prescription first. Which I did. I took it to a pharmacy.

RUTH   Why didn't *he* get the—

Claudie shrugs and continues.

CLAUDIE   I stand in line. I hand the paper to the pharmacist and he says in a loud voice: "What is this for?"

Beat.

"Crabs," I half mumble. "Crabs!" he repeats back. (*In a loud voice*) Then the woman behind me. She's about—(*To Carl*) Probably your mother's age.

RUTH (*Trying to joke*)   Which is what—your age?

Claudie smiles.

CARL (*Joining the joke*)   No, Mom's a little younger.

Ruth laughs hard at this.

CLAUDIE   She taps me on the shoulder and says, though it says on the bottle to shower twice a day with it, she'd found three times was really needed, especially for the men. Because of all the folds and things. I'm serious. Then she stands and sort of mimes a penis—we're in the pharmacy—in line. Stands there—(*Claudie mimes this.*) And she says you have to really check all around it. Lift it up. Look here, there. She said either I should help or he should get his mother.

Laughter. The phone rings. Claudie goes and picks it up, listens for an instant, then:

(*Into phone*) Who? I'm sorry. (*She hangs up, goes back and sits down. To Carl*) It was your father.

Short pause. Music plays.

(*To Ruth*) So he gave you crabs.

Beat.

RUTH   So you ran into Paul.

CARL   Is "Paul" Monsieur Darc?

RUTH   That's right. She and Monsieur Darc have been going out together.

CARL   But Monsieur Darc is married.

RUTH (*Picking up the book on the table*)   What's this? The *Kama Sutra*? I didn't know you had this.

CLAUDIE I don't usually keep it out here.

CLAUDIE (*To Ruth*) Are you going out with Robert tonight?

She ignores the question.

Then you'll eat with us. Carl and I haven't eaten all day.

CARL Am I staying for—?

RUTH (*Suddenly standing*) Carl wants to hear my album. Let's put it on for him! (*Leans over Carl and rubs his head*) You little music lover, you.

CLAUDIE Ruth, please.

RUTH (*Surprised*) I wasn't . . .

Carl has managed to put on the album: an early Beethoven or Mozart.

RUTH How was Le Louvre? Did you show him the pickup room? Sh—sh. That's me. Hear me?

They listen. Phone rings again. Claudie hesitates, then goes and answers it.

CLAUDIE (*Into phone*) Hello? Yes. One moment. (*Covers the receiver*) It's your mother, Carl.

Carl stands and goes to the phone. Music plays.

CARL (*Into phone*) Hello? Yes, I had a great time. Incredible art. (*Beat*) What time is it now? (*Looks at his watch*) Actually we were all about to start making dinner. The whole gang's here. A French dinner. Monsieur Melville is supervising.

Claudie and Ruth start making background noise of a group of students together. Carl nods to them— "Louder."

Sorry, Mom, I can't hear. (*To the room*) Hey everyone could you keep it down?

They don't.

What? (*Into phone*) Sorry. I have to go. Monsieur Melville needs my help with something! Bye!!

Hangs up. The others are quiet. Music plays. Silence.

CLAUDIE Don't upset your parents, Carl. You shouldn't do that.

Phone rings again.

(*Into phone*) Hello? (*Holds out phone*) It's your father.

With music playing, Carl takes the phone.

CARL (*Hesitates, then into phone*) Dad?

Carl says nothing. Shouting from the phone. He listens, then after a while, with the shouting continuing, he just hangs up. He sits back on the sofa. Claudie and Ruth don't know what to say.

RUTH (*Referring to the music*) That's me, too.

Beat.

(*Holding up the* Kama Sutra) Can I borrow this sometime?

CARL (*To Claudie*) I want to stay here.

CLAUDIE Think what you're doing.

CARL (*Yells*) I know what I'm doing!

Claudie is taken aback by this outburst.

CLAUDIE (*After a glance at Ruth, who still has her head in the book*) You're a wonderful boy. (*She reaches for his hand.*) We've had a lot of fun.

Beat.

You're more than a boy . . . but is it worth it, Carl?

CARL It is.

He refuses her hand. She looks at Ruth, who looks up and nods as if to say, "Tell him."

CLAUDIE You've been so—good to be with. I've enjoyed myself so much. Thank you.

Beat.

RUTH Claudie . . .

CLAUDIE (*Looks at Ruth, then:*) Ruth is right. I should tell you.

CARL Tell me what?

CLAUDIE Monsieur Darc and I—Monsieur Darc, your mathematics teacher and I—we had an argument this week, Carl . . . an awful argument. And we agreed not to see each other—again. See each other—as we have been seeing each other, I mean. I was hurt by this. Very hurt, Carl. I needed someone. Last night I needed some . . . I don't love you.

The phone starts to ring.

RUTH (*Referring to the music*) Maybe. I should turn this (*off*)—

CLAUDIE No.

She looks at Carl and starts to cry. Carl just looks at her, confused. Speaking over the ringing phone.

(*Sniffling*) That's not totally true. What I've just said . . . I . . . (*Rubs her sniffling nose*) I have hated myself today. Whenever I've allowed myself to think—what do you think you're doing, Claudie, he's . . . I have hated myself. Please go home.

No one moves. Carl stares at Claudie, then:

CARL   I'm staying here.

Phone has stopped ringing.

RUTH   (*Suddenly standing*)   What about wine? We should have wine if we're having dinner.

CLAUDIE   (*Wiping her eyes*)   There are bottles in the—

RUTH   I know where you keep it.

She goes off into the kitchen. Carl has watched her go.

CARL   (*To say something*)   Ruth looks so different. Than this morning. (*He hands her his handkerchief.*) In that dress. It's like she's another person. Like she's—beautiful. I suppose she is. Before I didn't think she was beautiful at all.

CLAUDIE   (*Blowing her nose now into the handkerchief*)   Women change. And there is a lesson in life, young man, that you will learn something like one or two billion more times.

She smiles and winks at him and hands him back his handkerchief. Phone rings again. They let it ring. Claudie sighs, breathes deeply and goes and turns up the music, then sits next to Carl on the sofa. The phone stops ringing.

CLAUDIE   What will he do to you?

He puts her hand on his leg. Ruth enters with a bottle of wine and a corkscrew.

RUTH   Here's the wine. Now shouldn't we have our man here open it? It is a man's thing to do.

CLAUDIE   "Please, sir—could you help us girls?"

He takes the bottle and starts to open it.

RUTH   Look at those muscles, Claudie.

CLAUDIE   I'm looking.

RUTH   Us girls couldn't do that.

CLAUDIE (*Pushing the joke*)   No-o-o-o.

Cork pops.

CARL   What shall it be, ladies ? (*Holds up the bottle*) Red or—
(*Picks up the crabs medicine*)—white?

The women are disgusted.

RUTH   For a minute there I forgot he was thirteen.

CLAUDIE (*"Correcting" her*) Twelve.

He pours. Music plays. Ruth pauses as she hears herself play.

CLAUDIE   Did you call Robert and tell him about the crabs?

RUTH   Why would I—?

Beat.

   I did. And he knew. He's known.

*The music ends and there is applause on the record. Claudie and then
Carl join in the applause.*

   It's the only record we've made so far. The only piece. The
rest of the album's other groups—

CLAUDIE (*To Carl*)   I was there. I was in that audience.
(*Listening to the applause*) There—that's me.

RUTH (*Getting the joke*)   Shut up. (*She smiles.*)

Applause on the record ends. Claudie goes to turn it off.

CARL   Can we play it again?

64

Claudie starts it again.

RUTH It was quite a night, wasn't it? Everything I'd dreamed of in my clean kitchen in Montclair, New Jersey.

The music continues; they listen.

CLAUDIE I'd never seen an all-girl string quartet before. It seemed really strange, you know. Good but strange. Like—I don't know.

RUTH (*Picking up the album cover*) Hélène is the real beauty. Beautiful red hair. That's red hair (*photo in black and white*). The cellist.

Carl looks at the photo.

CLAUDIE Carl was saying he thinks you're beautiful, Ruth.

Carl is embarrassed.

CARL Why did you—?

RUTH (*At the same time*) When did—?

CLAUDIE (*Continuing*) When you were—(*Gestures*) How you look now. Isn't that right?

He says nothing.

RUTH You've put him on the spot.

CLAUDIE (*Back to the concert*) I went with Paul. (*To Carl*) Monsieur Darc. And his wife. As sort of a teachers' group. And he said he had never even seen a female cellist before. (*To Carl*) They're hardly in orchestras.

RUTH Women.

CLAUDIE You never see them. (*Back to Ruth*) And just watching Hélène play, with her thighs, Paul said, wrapped

65

around it—it was, he said, one of the most sensual things he'd ever seen. Or heard.

Beat.

He said this to both me and his wife.

RUTH   When I left Monclair and my husband and my baby—

Carl turns on hearing this.

CLAUDIE (*Explaining*)   She left her baby.

RUTH (*Explaining more*)   My mother-in-law convinced me she'd be a better mother. (*Continuing her story*) My husband laughed in my face. Going to Paris? For Christ's sake, girl, what do you want? I said what I wanted is . . .

Beat.

I'm sure I said something stupid. Something I'd heard. Something I don't believe in anymore. Because I suppose I didn't know.

Beat.

But then came that night. (*Gestures toward the album. Pause*)

CARL (*Getting it. To Claudie*)   That's when she knew why she—

CLAUDIE   I understood.

Beat.

He beat her, Carl.

RUTH   I hit him too. Sometimes I hit him first. I don't blame him for that. I didn't leave for that.
   Let's not hear any more.

Claudie picks up the needle again and sets it on the end of Ruth's "cut." So we hear only the applause again. They listen to the applause for a moment. Ruth has picked up the Kama Sutra *again.*

Claudie begins to put on more music. As she does:

CLAUDIE I'd never let a man hit me.

RUTH (*Taking a cigarette from the pack*) Cigarette?

CLAUDIE Please. (*Hands her one*)

CARL I'd love to come and hear you play.

CLAUDIE Carl has been learning about music. His family doesn't listen to music. So he's practically a virgin.

Beat.

Practically.

Beat.

I've promised to take him to *The Magic Flute.*

RUTH When I was about your age. How old is he?

CLAUDIE Fifteen.

RUTH I was fourteen. I got—I asked for and I got a recording of *The Magic Flute* for Christmas.

CARL How did you know even to ask for—?

RUTH I just did. (*Continuing*) I played it over and over in my room. On my little portable plastic record player.

Claudie nods. She knows the type.

My friends, they were only interested in—(*Shrugs*) Elvis Presley? I don't know. In all sorts of things I wasn't interested in at all. That I thought were stupid. That I still think are stupid. My ex—He loved that stuff. He made me

67

dance to it with him. The son of a bitch even laughed at me when I practiced. What's that going to get you? What is that—*about*? I felt like a freak in that house. And maybe I was. I'll play for you sometime. (*Smiles at Carl*)

CARL   Thank you.

CLAUDIE   Robert, I thought, plays the guitar like Elvis . . .

RUTH   I wasn't interested in his guitar playing.

They laugh, calm down, then quietly:

Robert and his little tiny friends (*his crabs*). Look at this. I was looking through this (*the* Kama Sutra). There's—(*Finds the reference*) "the widely opened position." That's me. Completely open.

CLAUDIE   I don't think I've read any of the text. I bought it for the pictures. (*Looks at the book*)

RUTH   (*Reads*)   "The yawning position." That's me with my ex. "The position of the wife of Indra."

CLAUDIE   What is that one? The wife one.

RUTH   (*Reads*)   "When she places her thighs with her legs doubled on them upon her sides and thus engages in congress."

Beat.

"This is learnt only by practice."

Beat.

CLAUDIE   Jesus.

RUTH   (*Continues reading*)   "When a woman forcibly holds in her yoni the lingam after it is in, it is called the 'mare's position.' This too is learnt by practice only and is chiefly found among the women of the Andra country."

CLAUDIE (*Turning to Carl*)   Are you staying the night or . . . ?

CARL   I don't know.

RUTH (*Reads*)   "When a man supports himself against a wall, and the woman, sitting on his hands joined together and held underneath her, throws her arms around his neck, and putting her thighs alongside his waist, moves herself by her feet, which are touching the wall against which the man is leaning, it is called the 'suspended congress.'"

Beat.

CLAUDIE (*Unable to visualize this*)   What???

Ruth hands her the book, pointing at the page.

CLAUDIE   There's no picture?

RUTH   Not for that one.

Carl sits uncomfortably between them.

CLAUDIE (*Reads to herself*)   "When a man against a wall—" Carl, come over to the wall.

Stands, pulling up Carl. He hesitates. He follows her; she reads.

"Against a wall." (*She positions Carl against the wall.*) "Woman, sitting on his hands" . . . (*As she joins his hands together:*) Like this. (*Reads*) "Underneath her." (*She starts to climb up onto his hands.*) Pick me up. Carl. That's right. "Arms around the neck—" Ruth, could you hold the book?

Ruth takes the book.

69

"Thighs alongside his waist." (*To Ruth*) Like this you think?

Ruth holds out the book for Claudie to read as she starts to climb onto Carl, whose back is pressed against the wall.

"Moves herself by her feet." (*She is on him, and starts to move her feet.*)
Is that right? Did I skip something?

She looks to Ruth, moves her feet. Carl is trying to keep his balance.

(*To Carl*) Keep holding. (*To Ruth*) What does that—? (*To Carl*) Carl, you're letting me—Carl!

They stumble away from the wall. Claudie calls to Ruth for help; tries to push him back to the wall, until finally, as Claudie screams, Carl and she fall, laughing.
Carl takes this chance quickly to kiss her—the first time he has. She realizes this and kisses him back.

CLAUDIE (*Not a question*) You are staying tonight.

RUTH I think I should go. I—

CLAUDIE No, no, not yet. Please, we were going to eat. What happened to eating?

RUTH I don't think anyone's hungry. I'm not hungry.

CLAUDIE You should eat. Remember you're eating for more than one now.

RUTH Christ.

CARL (*Not understanding*) What, is Ruth—?

CLAUDIE For five or six hundred or more now.

Carl realizes that it's another joke about the crabs.

Then let's at least open another bottle of wine. Drink up.

CARL (*The wine bottle is still half full.*)   We haven't finished—

CLAUDIE   We will! I'll get the wine!

Claudie goes to the kitchen. Music plays.
Ruth and Carl say nothing for a moment, but they smile at each
other.

RUTH (*Finally*)   That—(*when Carl was against the wall*)—was
funny.

Carl nods.

Short pause, then:

CARL (*As if explaining everything*)   She's my teacher.

Beat.

They burst out laughing.

Beat.

RUTH   Claudie was telling me about a student of hers who
was going to be a poet.

This stops him.

So that's you.

Beat.

You don't have any of your poems—?

CARL   I don't know what I'll be.

RUTH   Claudie has tons of poetry books.

CARL   I know. I've seen.

CLAUDIE (*Entering with wine and cheese*)   Where's our man (*to*
open the wine)?

71

RUTH   Claudie should show you her writing.

CLAUDIE (*Protesting*)   Ruth, I'm not going to show—

RUTH (*To Carl*)   She's writing a novel.

CARL   You never said—

CLAUDIE (*Over this*)   What literature teacher hasn't tried to write a novel? Choose some music.

RUTH   Show him. He'd be interested—

CLAUDIE   Carl, you choose—

CARL   I don't know what to—

RUTH (*Over this*)   You want to know what it's about? It's about—

CLAUDIE   Don't tell him! (*Covers his ears*) It sounds stupid talking about it.

Beat.

RUTH   It's interesting.

CARL   I'm sure it—

CLAUDIE   Open the wine, young man. (*Trying to change the subject and make a joke*) Earn your keep. Make up for your inability to perform the suspended congress or whatever it was called in the book.

No response. Carl and Ruth just look at her.

(*To Ruth*) Why did you bring that up?

RUTH (*To Carl*)   I'll choose some music.

She takes the job away from a reluctant Carl. She will put something quiet on—piano music.

72

Pause.

CLAUDIE (*Finally*)   Okay. Every student should get at least once the chance to laugh at his teacher. (*She heads off to her bedroom.*)

CARL   I won't laugh.

The music is on. Claudie returns with a box of papers and sets it down. Carl has just opened the bottle of wine.

CLAUDIE (*Holding out her glass to Carl*)   I need a drink for this.

He pours.

It takes place, of course, in the Middle Ages.

CARL   Why "of course"?

RUTH   Because it's about—

CLAUDIE   Sh—sh.

Beat.

RUTH   She's done a lot of research and—

CLAUDIE   Ruth.

Beat.

A specific period: November 1429 to about the next March 1430. Four and a half months. Mostly in a large barn; it's actually a workshop attached to a convent—outside Paris. A group of women, mostly nuns—but nuns at this time, it's complicated. Here is where they paint. You've seen—I showed you a couple today, Carl—the painted manuscripts, called illuminated manuscripts. Did you know that many of these—all of which are attributed to monks, to this monastery or that order of monks—were in truth painted by women?

73

Beat.

Sort of "farmed out" art. To different convents—which got no credit but a little money from the monks—who got a lot more from—whomever was paying.

Beat.

So some of the nuns here—well, their major skill was painting and so pretty much anyone could be a nun if they painted well—that was *the* qualification—so you could in fact *be* other things. You couldn't be married, but you could have men. You could have children. But you were a nun.

Beat.

Into this barn, one day, comes a man in a suit of armor. A short man. Visor down, staggering under the weight of the metal. The women, seeing the soldier and fearing the worst, try and flee, but a voice calls out from inside the armor:
"Stop. Please. I'm not here to hurt you."
And the soldier falls to the dirt ground. One of the women goes to him, hesitantly, and in removing the helmet realizes—the man is a woman.

RUTH The most famous woman—

CLAUDIE Jeanne d'Arc.

Beat.

Let me backtrack for a second. By the autumn of 1429, Jeanne d'Arc was without doubt the most famous woman in France—in the world maybe, but certainly in France. She'd helped us capture Orléans, and helped crown the Dauphin. Because of this her movements are well documented—part of history. A day-by-day account of what she did, where she was—can be put together. (*She sips, then:*) Until

74

November 1429. And for the next four months. With the sole exception of a single visit to Orléans, where she was seen by others only at a distance, and from a balcony. Except for this—Jeanne's whereabouts are unknown. As are the reasons for her disappearance. All this is true.

Beat.

So it is Jeanne d'Arc on this dirt ground, in the convent's barn. And why is she here, Carl? Because—she's pregnant.

Phone rings. They hesitate, then Claudie nods to Ruth, who gets up and answers it.

RUTH (*Into phone*)   Hello? It's Ruth. (*She turns to Claudie.*) It's Paul.

Carl is relieved, having of course thought that it was his father.

CLAUDIE   I'm busy.

Ruth looks at her.

I am busy.

RUTH (*Into phone*)   She's busy. (*Hangs up*)

CLAUDIE (*Another drink, then:*)   The Maid of Orléans, the virgin princess, this woman whose very purity is the definition of France—has fallen.

Beat.

She is taken in. Allowed to sleep in the hay. She grows larger. For a long time she won't speak. The women, one day, get her to pose, naked, pregnant, for a painting of the Virgin Mary. They needed a model.

Beat.

She will say nothing of the father. She is still obsessed with her own purity. "What does that"—her bulging stomach—asks one of the women, "have to do with purity?" This particular woman was a very fine painter and a nun in name only.

Beat.

Finally—and I'm skipping way ahead now—the Dauphin's people find her. That's when she has to go to Orléans and hide behind the railing on the balcony.

Beat.

The Dauphin's people are shocked. They predict the fall of France. Scholars are brought in and there is a movement to declare it an immaculate conception and the child of God. The brother—or sister—of Jesus. The men debate this, and the debate takes two months. Meanwhile Jeanne is allowed to return to the barn and the nuns. And there, in March 1430, she gives birth, with profound pain, to a baby girl.

Short pause.

The next day she puts her armor back on and returns to the Dauphin's side, where she stayed, until being captured and burnt at the stake.

Beat.

It's a story about a lot of things, but mostly I think it's about a woman who risks everything to have a child she knows she doesn't want.

Beat.

I've been pregnant three times. But I have no child.

Pause.

(*Quietly*) The last was your mathematics teacher's. (*She fiddles with the pages of the manuscript.*) It's not finished. (*She closes the box top, and suddenly, to change the subject and mood,*

she grabs the Kama Sutra, *quickly finds a page and reads.*)
"When after congress has begun the woman places one of
her legs on her lover's shoulder and stretches the other
out—"

Carl starts to open the box of papers.

CLAUDIE Don't read it.

*Carl closes the top. Ruth, who is still by the albums, suddenly holds
one up.*

RUTH (*Showing Claudie*) Claudie?

CLAUDIE (*Smiling*) Why not? He knows everything else about
us.

Carl is curious now.

RUTH (*To Carl*) You heard this? "Les Djinns Singers."

CARL No, who—?

RUTH My brother gave this to me as a going-away present.
He meant it as a joke, but we love it, don't we?

CLAUDIE (*Taking the album and reading the title*) "Sixty French
Girls Can't Be Wrong!"

As Claudie puts it on:

CARL Why is it (*here*)—?

RUTH My record player's been broken for—

CLAUDIE (*Reading the back of the album*) "From Paris come
these sixty princesses, to raise their voices in exuberant and
sentimental song in a dozen varied selections."

RUTH (*Jumps up and reads*) "What makes these renditions all
the more outstanding is the fact that the entire assemblage
consists of"—

77

BOTH   —"jeune filles"—

CLAUDIE   —"between the ages of thirteen and sixteen!"

RUTH   Your age, Carl!

CLAUDIE   "Each youngster was especially auditioned and selected on the basis of personal qualification and aptitude, and after an—unusually exacting audition." Bite your tongue, Ruth.

Claudie puts the needle down on the song "Oui Oui Oui"—sung by these sixty jeune filles. It is silly and kitsch. As soon as the music starts or just a fraction before, Claudie and Ruth form a "line" and mouth along. Doing a dance number they have worked out— obviously they have done this many times before.
Carl watches, smiling. The women can barely keep a straight face.

CLAUDIE (*As they dance*)   I think we've been alone together too many Saturday nights!

As the song plays, Carl has picked up the album to read it. Suddenly Claudie hurries to her bedroom.

CLAUDIE (*Rushing off*)   I'll be right back. Right back.

RUTH   I know what she's going to get.

As the song plays, Ruth opens a small drawer in a table and takes out a small bag of marijuana and some wrappers.

RUTH (*To Carl*)   Do you smoke grass?

Claudie runs out of her bedroom putting on white socks. She has another pair for Ruth.

CLAUDIE (*Explaining*)   To make us—jeune—(*Sees what Ruth is doing, almost says something, then doesn't*) Sixty-two French girls can't be wrong.

RUTH (*Taking the socks*)   I'm not French.

CLAUDIE In spirit you are! (*Then she has to say something.*) He doesn't smoke dope.

RUTH How do you know? (*To Carl*) You smoke dope?

CARL Sure.

Song continues. Ruth has put her white socks on and grabs Carl and dances with him. Claudie puts on her socks. As she does, she watches the two dance. Ruth starts to get quite close to Carl.

CLAUDIE (*Finally, after having seen enough*) Ruth, stop it. That's enough. (*To Carl*) Come here.

CARL There is a poem I could read. I have a copy— It's in my—

Takes a piece of paper out of his pocket.

CLAUDIE You have one of your poems with you, Carl? Why didn't you say—?

CARL (*Reads*)
   "Rhythms silent and—"

CLAUDIE Wait, Carl.

She hurries and turns down the music.

CARL (*Reads*)

   "Rhythms silent and frail
   of delicate air
   to catch the curling of hair.

   "Voice crisp and curt,
   O delicate voice,
   curling the catching air.

   "Silent hands
   catch the delicate rhythms
   from the frail hair,
   the silent and the frail hair."

79

Beat

RUTH (*To Claudie*)   Is it about you?

CARL   It's why I stayed back. Last night. In the toilet. To show it to you. So you might tell me what you think. There's more . . .

He hands her the poem.

RUTH   I'll get my fiddle. I feel like playing.
     I'll be right back.

She goes.

CLAUDIE   (*While looking at the poem*)   She doesn't play for everyone.

CARL   I'm flattered. Let's put the sixty French girls back on—

CLAUDIE   I love the poem. Thank you. It was brave of you to show it to me.

She looks at him, smiles, pushes his hair back.

     God I wish I could cut this off.

She kisses him, as Carl's FATHER, *a man in his forties, enters from the hallway, at first unseen.*

Carl turns and sees his father.

CARL   (*In shock*)   Father—

FATHER   The door was open.

CLAUDIE   Monsieur—

FATHER   Madame Melville. "Madame" with no husband. I spoke with the headmaster.

The music plays.

Carl, let's go.

He doesn't move.

Let's go, Carl.

Ruth enters behind him with her violin. Then Father goes to Carl and with neither saying a word, he reaches around and picks Carl up around the waist and begins carrying him out like a child.

Carl, without words or sound, fights, kicks like a little boy having a tantrum. As they struggle, Carl kicks the sofa, kicks objects off a table.

The two women can barely look. Claudie suddenly tries to stop the music—and drags the needle over the record, scratching it.

Now there is only silence as Father and son struggle. Only their breathing is heard, until finally, after a great effort, Father carries his child off.

Pause.

Neither woman says anything. Ruth begins absentmindedly to pluck her violin strings.

Lights shift and Carl returns and speaks to the audience, as the women slowly fade away. He carries a suit jacket.

CARL I was taken out of the ironically named American School immediately, and arrangements were made to send me back to Ohio to live with my aunts.

Beat.

I saw Mme. Melville again only once. The night before my departure, Father and Mother took me to a restaurant for dinner. I requested something on the Left Bank, near the Sorbonne. Father was suspicious. But Mother, already upset that I was leaving, and missing me terribly, agreed to whatever I wished.

81

Beat.

We ordered. I went to wash my hands in the WC, and kept running. I figured Father would know where I went, but I also figured he wouldn't bring Mother with him, nor could he leave her in the restaurant alone. This was France, after all. So he'd drive her home first, and this gave me time.

Beat.

She wore a short, tight, black dress.

Claudie enters in a black dress. She turns and lets Carl zipper her up.

I wore a suit that I thought made me look old.

Claudie helps him on with his suit jacket.

When I arrived, she told me she had a date for that night, so I couldn't stay long. We sat together on the sofa. She put on music.

Claudie puts on an album.

CARL What are you—?

CLAUDIE *The Magic Flute.*

It is the "Papagena! Papagena!" duet. They listen. Claudie takes off her shoes and curls up next to him. He looks at her.

CARL What are they (*saying*)—?

CLAUDIE They love each other. They want to be together.

Beat.

Listen.

She touches him to get him focusing on a moment in the music.
They listen.
She touches his leg, apparently by accident. He notices.

Excuse me.

She moves her hand. She looks up at him, then away.
Doorbell. He looks at her, then to the audience.

CARL (*To audience*) She asked me to stay until after she'd
gone. She said she didn't want Paul, Monsieur Darc, my
math teacher, to see me here.

Silence.

Claudie leans over and slips on her shoes. She stands and holds out
her hand so Carl can steady her as she adjusts her shoes.
She looks at him, then turns and looks at the back of her skirt.

CLAUDIE Is it smooth?

He nods.

No wrinkles?

He shakes his head.
She straightens the skirt anyway.
Slowly she walks toward the door. He watches her walk. She again
runs her hand along her behind, to straighten out any wrinkles.
Carl continues to watch.
As she approaches the door, she turns back to him and, with only
the tips of her fingers, waves good-bye and is gone.
From the hallway we hear the door opening, a brief conversation,
and the door closing, and the music goes out.

Pause.

CARL Years later. And years and years ago. When I was
twenty-four, I ran into a friend from my Paris days. And he
told me Mme. Melville had died.

Beat.

Of cancer, he thought.

Pause.

CARL (*To the air*)   May I see that good-bye one more time?

Beat.

Claudie returns (there is no sound of the door opening). She goes to the sofa and sits, taking off her shoes and placing them just where they were before.
   She leans against Carl.
   She leans over and slips on her shoes. She stands and holds out her hand so Carl can steady her as she adjusts her shoes.
   She looks at him, then turns and looks at the back of her skirt.

CLAUDIE   Is it smooth?

He nods.

   No wrinkles?

He shakes his head.
   She straightens the skirt anyway.
   Slowly she walks toward the door. He watches her walk. She again runs her hand along her behind, to straighten out any wrinkles.
   Carl continues to watch.
   As she approaches the door, she turns back to him and, with only the tips of her fingers, waves good-bye and is gone.
   From the hallway we hear the door opening, a brief conversation, and the door closing. This time the music continues.

Pause.

End of play.

THE GENERAL
FROM
AMERICA

For Robert Marx

The General from America was first performed by the
Royal Shakespeare Company on July 17, 1996, at the Swan
Theatre, Stratford-on-Avon. The cast was as follows:

BENEDICT ARNOLD   James Laurenson

PEGGY ARNOLD   Jay McInnes

HANNAH ARNOLD   Rachel Joyce

MAJOR JOHN ANDRE   Adam Godley

SIR HENRY CLINTON   John Woodvine

ALEXANDER HAMILTON   David Tennant

GENERAL GEORGE WASHINGTON   Corin Redgrave

MAJOR STEPHEN KEMBLE   Stephen Boxer

JOSEPH REED   Benny Young

TIMOTHY MATLACK   Jon Rake

COLONEL SIMCOE   Nathaniel Duncan

YOUNG WOMAN   Jacquelyn Yorke

MRS. HENRY CLINTON   Jan Chappell

VAN WART   Simeon Defoe

PAULING   Andrew Hesker

MR. ROBINSON   Owen Oakeshott

MAID   Emma Poole

Other parts played by members of the company.

Director   Howard Davies
Designer   William Dudley
Lighting Designer   Mark Henderson
Music   Ilona Sekacz
Fights   Terry King
Sound   Martin Slavin
Music Director   Michael Tubbs
Assistant Director   Simon Nicholson
Dialect Work   Joan Washington
Company Voice Work   Andrew Wade and Barbara Houseman

Stage Manager   Maggie Mackay
Deputy Stage Manager   Rosalind Morgan-Jones
Assistant Stage Manager   Joyce Green

CHARACTERS

BENEDICT ARNOLD

PEGGY ARNOLD, his wife

HANNAH ARNOLD, his sister

MAJOR JOHN ANDRE

SIR HENRY CLINTON

ALEXANDER HAMILTON

GENERAL GEORGE WASHINGTON

MAJOR STEPHEN KEMBLE

JOSEPH REED

TIMOTHY MATLACK

COLONEL SIMCOE

YOUNG WOMAN behind the curtain

MRS. HENRY CLINTON

VAN WART, a skinner

PAULING, a skinner

OFFICERS, ORDERLIES, etc.

The following is based on true events.

SCENE ONE

British-occupied New York City. 1779.

Small room in a British Officers' Club. A small curtained area, to be used as a makeshift stage. A chair. The room is fairly dark.
    SIR HENRY CLINTON, *fifty, commander in chief of the British Army in North America, sits in the chair facing the "stage." Around him are* THREE OFFICERS. *They watch a recitation of a poem written and performed by* MAJOR JOHN ANDRE, *twenty-nine, a deputy adjutant general. All drink and smoke.*
    Andre stands before the curtain, reading the poem, which is called "The Frantic Lover."

ANDRE
    And shall then another embrace thee my Fair!
    Must envy still add to the pangs of Despair!
    Shall I live to behold the reciprocal bliss!
    Death, death is a refuge, Elysium to this!

OFFICER   He must be talking about New York.

Laughter.

Andre nods to an ORDERLY *by the stage, who now pulls open the curtain. One Officer sh—shs the others.*

A YOUNG WOMAN *is revealed. She stands in a tableau vivant that has some relation to the poem being read. After a moment, the curtain closes and Andre continues.*

ANDRE
    The star of the evening now bids thee retire
    Accurs'd be its Orb and extinguished its fire!
    For it shows me my rival prepared to invade
    Those charms which at once I admired and obey'd.
    Far off each forbidding Incumbrance is thrown
    And Sally thy beauties no more are thy own.

Another nod to the Orderly, the curtain is opened, and the Young Woman is in another tableau vivant—though she has now taken off some of her clothes.

Pause. No one says anything. Only Sir Henry turns away and watches Andre instead of the stage. The curtain closes and Andre continues.

Thy coyness too flies as love brings to thy View
A frame more ecstatic than Saint ever knew!
And yet I behold thee tho' longing to die
Approach the new Heaven with a tear and a sigh!
For oh! the fond sigh midst Enjoyment will stray,
And a Tear is the Tribute which Rapture must pay.
Still, still dost thou tremble that pleasure to seek,
Which pants in thy Bosom and glows in they cheek.

Curtain opens. The Young Woman is now naked above the waist, and again in a pose.

No one says anything; they watch, except for Sir Henry, who again turns back to Andre, smiling. Curtain closes.

Here Conquest must pause tho' it ne'er can be cloy'd
To view the rich plunder of beauty enjoy'd,
The tresses disheveled, the Bosom display'd,
And the Wishes of Years in a moment repaid.
A Thousand soft thoughts in thy fancy combine
A Thousand wild horrors assemble in Mine;
Relieve me kind death, shut the Scene from my View,
And Save me, oh save me, ere madness ensue!

The curtain opens one last time, and the Young Woman is now completely naked. In a melodramatic pose, she now holds a sword and a British flag, and she wears on her head a British officer's hat.

Pause.

Again silence for a while. Andre and Clinton share a smile as the other Officers watch the stage. Finally the curtain closes and Andre folds the paper he has been reading from—the show is over; everyone suddenly relaxes, though no one knows what to say. An awkward pause.

SIR HENRY (*Finally*)   Splendid poem.

The Officers burst out talking at once and at the same time congratulating John, praising him, etc. "Very nice!" "I've heard much worse in London." "And well performed!" "He's quite the actor." "I saw him on Monday in *She Stoops to Conquer*." "I want to see that." "I saw him last night."
    The Young Woman comes out from behind the curtain, a blanket around her shoulders. She hurries out—this has stopped all conversation as they watch.
    She passes MAJOR STEPHEN KEMBLE, *who is entering.*

KEMBLE   Sir Henry. If I may have a word.

An Officer holds up an empty glass: "Perhaps we should—" *Before he gets even a word out, they are heading off to find more to drink:* "We'll be in the next room, sir!" *One, nodding in the direction of the Young Woman:* "She's a good actress, don't you think?" "She'd do well in London."

Kemble stops Andre, who is heading out with the others.

Major Andre. If you wouldn't mind. This may interest you.

ANDRE (*To the Officers*)   Get me whatever. I'll catch up.

The Officers leave, talking. Sir Henry has reached out and taken Andre's hand.

SIR HENRY   What is it, Kemble? (*To Andre*) The men enjoyed that I think.

ANDRE   We need to keep up—their spirits.

Andre and Sir Henry laugh at the joke.

KEMBLE (*Over the laughter*) Sir Henry, we believe we've learned the source of the letter Major Andre received.

Beat.

ANDRE The man who signs himself "Monk"?

KEMBLE (*Ignoring Andre*) And we believe—no, we're certain—that the writer of the letter, our possible defector, is—General Benedict Arnold—

ANDRE Jesus Christ.

KEMBLE (*Over this*)—of the rebel army. Presently military governor of the city of Philadelphia. (*He continues his list.*) Hero of Saratoga. The most decorated and successful officer in the Continental army.

SIR HENRY (*Over the end of this*) I know who he is.

Pause. Sir Henry has let go of Andre's hand.

ANDRE Why would—?

KEMBLE (*Turns to Andre*) Arnold's duty in Philadelphia has been, shall we say, less than rewarding. It's become a mess down there, or so one hears. (*Beat. To Sir Henry*) The man's a bloody good soldier and, it seems, a terrible politician. He's being eaten alive. So I suppose it makes some sense for him to test the waters. Which is all I believe the letter attempts to do.

Short pause.

SIR HENRY You are sure—?

Kemble nods.

This is extraordinary.

He reaches for and takes Andre's hand again, and holds it now between his two hands.

KEMBLE   Yes, sir. I agree.

SIR HENRY (*Looking up at Andre*)   John . . .

ANDRE   Perhaps their so-called revolution has begun to devour itself. Like you said it would, sir. Congratulations.

SIR HENRY   It's one man.

ANDRE   The first, sir.

SIR HENRY   We'll see. Still it's good news.

KEMBLE   I believe we must write back at once, sir, and give him every encouragement.

SIR HENRY   Yes.

KEMBLE   And promise him? Whatever? (*To Andre*) Sorry, Major, to have interrupted. I understand you're performing now. *She Stoops to Conquer?*

Andre nods.

Good play. (*He turns to Sir Henry.*) By the way, the "Monk" he signs with, we believe, refers to a George Monk, general under Cromwell who changed sides. And for this action received from a grateful sovereign at least a dukedom. So—I don't suppose he's thinking cheap.

SIR HENRY   No.

Kemble turns to leave.

ANDRE (*Pulling his hand away from Sir Henry*)   One second, Stephen. (*To Sir Henry*) Sir, shouldn't I be the one responding?

KEMBLE   I don't think that's wise—

Sir Henry holds up his hand and cuts Kemble off. He wants to hear what Andre has to say.

ANDRE   He wrote to me. The letter's to me. It could spook the man if someone else—

KEMBLE (*Interrupting*)   He was obviously writing to the commander in chief. Somehow, maybe through mutual acquaintances in Philadelphia, he'd learned Andre's name. I doubt if—

ANDRE   We don't know that!

Kemble is taken aback by Andre's vehemence.

KEMBLE   You are just a name to get to Sir Henry!

ANDRE (*Over this, to Sir Henry*)   Sir, I ask permission to respond to the letter *I* received.

KEMBLE   Sir, Major Andre is not qualified to—

ANDRE   It's my letter!

KEMBLE   I run the service!

ANDRE   Sir Henry?

KEMBLE   General, please!

They both look to Sir Henry.

SIR HENRY   We must do the cautious thing. Keep it simple. Not get ahead of ourselves. (*Beat*) A man contemplating this—a general, he must be . . .

Beat. Andre stares at Sir Henry.

John has a point; General Arnold wrote to him.

KEMBLE   Sir, it requires a professional response—

SIR HENRY (*Over this*) For whatever reason, he did this. We don't know why. And I'm not about to guess. (*He looks at both men.*) It's not a question of rank. You're both . . . majors. John's now a major. And we know he's a very fine writer.

KEMBLE I don't see what that has to—

SIR HENRY Please, don't interrupt me. (*Beat*) Arnold must not be scared off. Too many cooks—as they say. Thank you, Major Kemble, I appreciate your hard work. You've done well.

Kemble doesn't move.

I said—thank you.

ANDRE I'll take the letter please, Stephen.

Kemble hands Andre the letter.

I'll copy you what I write, if you'd like. We're having drinks, if you . . .

KEMBLE No.

Kemble turns and leaves.
  Andre fiddles with the letter, then holds it up, amazed.

ANDRE Monk is Benedict Arnold. (*He shakes his head in disbelief.*)

SIR HENRY Kemble's probably right—he's just testing the waters. So let's not push him in, John. Wait until he jumps.

ANDRE I'll do my best.

Sir Henry stands for the first time in the scene, and begins to head off toward the bar.

Sir? Thank you.

Sir Henry stops, looks at Andre.

For once again showing such confidence in me. I owe you so much.

Sir Henry takes a good long look at Andre, then smiles, goes to him, puts his arm around him and gives him a big "fatherly" hug that is a little too big and lasts a little too long.

He lets him go, looks into Andre's eyes, then with his hand makes a stroke across Andre's cheek.

SIR HENRY Just don't disappoint me.

Sir Henry turns and goes out. Andre follows.

SCENE TWO

Philadelphia. Two weeks later. A public square. Night.

A drumroll, and a few men carrying lanterns enter, followed by the drummer. Upstage, in the shadows, a man has been hanged from a tree or scaffold.

Two of the men are JOSEPH REED, *forties, president of Pennsylvania, and* TIMOTHY MATLACK, *secretary of the Committee of Pennsylvania. They face an (unseen) crowd.*

REED (*To the crowd*) Quiet! Quiet!

The crowd does not quiet down. Reed turns to the drummer, who then plays a drumroll which quiets the crowd.

(*Addressing the crowd*) This man . . .

Gestures behind him, then looks to Matlack, who quickly whispers the man's name.

John Roberts, having been tried and convicted of loyalist sympathies, of corresponding with the enemy, of corruption and other crimes against the Commonwealth, has been duly hanged as a spy.

A few cheers from the crowd.

The Committee of Pennsylvania, as the legitimate
representative of the people, lays legal claim to all Roberts's
properties and monies and accepts Roberts's widow and—

He turns back to Matlack, who whispers; then:

—ten children into its bosom, wards of the state. May God
have mercy upon them. And may the Lord find the food to
feed them.

*Reed steps back. Another drumroll. Matlack steps forward, a list in
hand.*

MATLACK (*Reading from the list*)   By the action of the
committee, three more dwellings have been cleared. Space
in these comfortable houses will be assigned to homeless
families by lottery. (*Then next on the list*) Sick women and
children are now to be taken only to twenty-seven Market
Street. All medicine is now stored there. This to combat the
hoarding of medical supplies by some doctors. (*He looks up
from his list.*) Hoarding of medicine is a crime punishable by
death. (*Then next on the list*) The committee announces the
arrival of twelve wagons of grain from the west. Bread
rations shall be increased. The amount of increase shall be
posted.

He finishes the list, puts it away, looks at Reed, then continues.

The author of the unsigned attack upon the committee,
its president (*Nods toward Reed*) and this Commonwealth
which recently appeared in the *Evening Post* has been
revealed. (*Beat*) His name is Humphreys. Mr. Whitehead
Humphreys. He resides, I believe, on Front Street.
Number twelve.

Matlack is now finished; he turns to the drummer, who gives another roll.

REED (*Over the roll, to the crowd*)   Cut him down! (*He points to the hanged man.*) Drag him through our streets! Let him be stoned and spat upon! By those he has betrayed!

MATLACK (*Turns back and cries*)   Cut him down!

Drumroll continues as Reed and Matlack hurry off.

SCENE THREE

The next day.

Garden of the Penn Mansion (Benedict Arnold's residence), Philadelphia. Three chairs. A sunny afternoon.
    BENEDICT ARNOLD, *thirty-eight, though looking older, enters with* HANNAH ARNOLD, *his sister, thirty-five. Arnold limps on his wounded leg; Hannah helps him to a chair and he sits. Off—sounds of people arriving.*
    ALEXANDER HAMILTON, *twenty-three, secretary to George Washington; Joseph Reed; and* PEGGY ARNOLD, *Benedict's young wife, enter. Peggy is nineteen, though she looks considerably younger, more like sixteen.*

ARNOLD (*Trying to stand*)   Colonel Hamilton.

HAMILTON (*Over this*)   Don't get up, please, General.

ARNOLD (*Over this*)   How is our commander in chief?

HAMILTON   As well as can be expected.

ARNOLD (*Not listening; continues to introduce*)   My sister. Colonel Alexander Hamilton. You've met my wife?

HAMILTON   Yes, just inside—

ARNOLD (*To Peggy, who is helping Arnold sit back down in the chair*)   Colonel Hamilton recently married, as well.

PEGGY   General Schuyler's daughter. I know.

HAMILTON   Who sends regards.

ARNOLD   The daughter does? (*He laughs at his joke, then winks at Peggy.*)

HAMILTON (*Taken aback*)   No, the General does, sir.

ARNOLD   Ahhh! Now that's explained! (*He smiles.*)

HAMILTON (*Over this*)   He is a great admirer. (*He nods toward Arnold.*) You must know that, he tells everyone—you are our greatest field general.

ARNOLD   Look at the competition. That's hardly a compliment.

HANNAH   We expected you earlier. May I take your hat?

ARNOLD (*Over this, to Peggy*)   I've told you about Schuyler—

PEGGY   Like a father to you.

ARNOLD (*Over this, to Hamilton*)   What can I get you? Take Mr. Hamilton's hat, Hannah.

PEGGY   Sit down, please.

Peggy sits next to Arnold. There is only one remaining chair.

Reed has been completely ignored and stands awkwardly to one side.

HAMILTON (*Hesitating to sit*)   And Mr. Reed?

ARNOLD (*Ignoring him*)   You don't mind sitting outside—?

PEGGY   It's terribly hot in the house.

HAMILTON   I don't mind. It's lovely. There's a nice breeze.

Hamilton, feeling awkward because Reed is left standing, turns to Reed.

Mr. Reed was kind enough to escort me—

ARNOLD (*Turns to Reed*) Mr. Reed, are you joining us?

Beat.

HAMILTON Is there another chair?

ARNOLD Peggy, do we have another chair for Mr. Reed?

PEGGY I don't think so.

ARNOLD Pity.

Awkward pause.

(*Taking Peggy's hand*) Is she as lovely as you've heard, Mr. Hamilton?

HAMILTON It is our good fortune that I'm now married, sir. (*He laughs.*)

ARNOLD You're not that handsome. (*He smiles. To Peggy*) Is he?

PEGGY I'm sure his new rich wife thinks so.

HANNAH Is Mr. Reed staying? I'll bring tea. How many cups—?

REED I came only to deliver Colonel Hamilton. That is now achieved. (*Beat*) My regards, Colonel, to General Washington—

ARNOLD (*Over the end of this, to Reed*) What crimes do the Committee of Pennsylvania accuse me of today? (*He laughs at his joke and turns back to the others.*)

REED That depends—upon what crimes you have committed today, General.

Beat.

ARNOLD (*To Hamilton*) For him, we sacrifice. We die. It makes no sense. Each morning I wake up and think: Am I mad?

REED You haven't died yet. I keep waiting.

ARNOLD (*Over the end of this*)   You arrogant bastard, I gave a leg for you people!

REED   And *that* leg I honor. It's the hand you've got in our pocket that I abhor!

ARNOLD   I am an honest man!

REED (*To Hamilton*)   Read him the charges.

HAMILTON   Please, I've listened to you! You've had your say!

REED (*Over this*)   Tell him what he's done!

ARNOLD (*Nearly bolting to his feet*)   What I've done! Where to even begin with what you've done! (*To Hamilton*) Just last night—have you heard what took place again last night?

REED (*Over this*)   You can't defend the writer!

HAMILTON (*To Reed*)   What took place last—?

ARNOLD   First the offices of the *Evening Post* were attacked again by his thugs.

REED   They are not thugs! They are good citizens of Philadelphia!

ARNOLD (*Over this, continuing*)   For publishing an editorial, this time critical of Mr. Reed's committee's effort to seize all women and children of Loyalists who have departed the city.

PEGGY (*Over this*)   I thought he was leaving—we have no more chairs!

REED (*To Arnold*)   We are afraid for their safety.

ARNOLD   Untrue. You want their homes.

REED   We are short of food.

ARNOLD This is true.

REED And they are women and children of traitors!

ARNOLD They are women and children!

REED (*Over this*) People are hungry—look in the streets. If you can get your face out of your own full table!

ARNOLD (*Over the end of this*) My soul is with the people in the streets!

REED (*To Hamilton*) Control your greed, General! That's all we ask!

ARNOLD As you attack our newspapers!

REED An overflow of liberty. Too much vigilance is better than too little. I am a radical, General Arnold. I will not shrink from that.

Beat.

ARNOLD And I am not? (*He looks around incredulously.*) Is this not my war too?

REED You do not wish me to answer that, sir. Mr. Hamilton, I've done my duty. I've spoken the truth. I've catalogued the crimes. And I've brought you to the criminal. What more can I do? Good day. Give my regards to our commander in chief and tell him, I pray for him. Daily. (*He turns and leaves.*)

Hannah has just entered with the tea.

HANNAH Should I show him out?

Arnold has turned away. Short pause.

HAMILTON I'm sorry, but what occurred last night? What— do you think occurred?

Arnold hesitates, hearing the correction, then:

ARNOLD Thugs—Mr. Reed's patriots—broke into the newspaper office I mentioned, which had had the audacity to criticize Mr. Reed's committee—in an unsigned article of course. How brave we've all become.

Hannah has begun to set out the tea. Peggy helps.

They beat the name of the author out of whomever happened to be there. A merchant, a Mr. Humphreys, I believe, is the writer. And then an even bigger mob was raised, went to Humphreys' house. He wasn't home, so they beat up his sister instead.

PEGGY I know the woman.

ARNOLD And a boarder, who happened to be a new member of Congress from Georgia. Thus is Mr. Reed's—liberty.

PEGGY (*To Hamilton*) The woman's a friend of my sister's. Small, frail woman.

ARNOLD (*Sitting back, closing his eyes*) They do not wish a revolution, Mr. Hamilton. They wish a civil war. But I am only a soldier. I do only what I'm told. My job now is to shoot Americans as they fight for food in the street.

Short pause. Tea is poured.

HAMILTON It will get better.

No response. Then Arnold opens his eyes and leans forward to take his tea.

ARNOLD (*Under his breath*) Will it?

Peggy takes his hand in hers. Silence. No one knows what to say. Above, a flock of geese is heard passing by.

Arnold shifts his weight; he is in some discomfort and pain. Peggy leans over and slowly lifts his bad leg up with effort. Arnold dramatically waves her off, and then with great effort and pain, and without help, he lifts his wounded leg onto the edge of Peggy's chair.

HAMILTON Allow me, sir, to help . . .

ARNOLD No. I bear my burden alone. I need no help. I have the sin of pride, sir. (*He stifles a groan, then adjusts his position. In pain*) So Reed has accused me of—? I'm sure you'll tell me all.

HAMILTON I've spent the morning taking his deposition, yes.

ARNOLD And what do you think?

HAMILTON I'm not here to think, sir. General Washington will review my reports, and he shall decide on the merits of this case. (*Beat*) The charges against you, sir, are serious. Civilians are being hanged for what you've been accused of. (*Beat*) I'm here now to learn what you'd like to say. To have in the record. (*Beat*) We can begin whenever you . . .

Arnold watches the birds, seemingly distracted and uninterested.

Perhaps Mrs. Arnold . . .

ARNOLD (*Watching the birds*) My wife will stay. She is my comfort.

Hannah turns to leave.

And my sister. Who has always stood at my side.

Hannah turns back.

HAMILTON I understand. (*He begins to set up a lap desk in preparation for taking notes.*)

PEGGY Would you like anything, Colonel?

HAMILTON I'm—

ARNOLD (*Before he can answer*) I don't know what you want from me. Or what you expect. I am a proud man; forgive me for that. And that is all I shall ask you to forgive me for.

HAMILTON (*Being handed a cake*) Perhaps if you address—

ARNOLD (*Interrupting*) I cannot plead for my honesty!

HAMILTON (*Continuing*) If you address the charges. Give us your own explanations. That will be enough.

Beat. Arnold looks at Peggy, then Hannah, then:

ARNOLD Go ahead. What is the first charge?

HAMILTON (*Balancing the cake, and papers, and lap desk*) Mr. Reed and the Committee of Pennsylvania claim—

ARNOLD (*Interrupting*) I have killed, I don't know, maybe forty men with these hands, Colonel—in this war. Our war. I have not been a general who stays on the high ground.

HAMILTON That is well known. And much admired.

ARNOLD Six, no, seven—with a sword. I know what the English claim: We cannot stand and take a bayonet run. That hasn't been the case with me, has it?

HAMILTON No, sir.

ARNOLD (*Turning to the women, who react to the gruesomeness of his story*) The sound, the feel of the blade hitting bone. That's something you don't forget. It's like a— (*He makes the sound.*) And if you hit the bone head on, it pushes you back a bit. Can knock you down. (*He demonstrates—the jerk reaction. To Hamilton*) That's if you plunge. (*He turns to*

Peggy, who is making faces, reacting to the gore.) She's a woman. (*To Hamilton*) If you swipe, you want to keep your wrist loose, forget the bone, and slice the muscle. Take the bugger down. Kill him when he's down. They beg with their eyes then. What's the first charge? (*Then without letting Hamilton answer*) It was seven. Not six. With the sword. I remember now. He was a boy. The seventh. Plunged it into his godforsaken face. Ridgefield. The seventh. (*Short pause*) Have you ever had to kill a man, Colonel?

HAMILTON   Me? No, I . . .

Arnold smiles, leans over and hits Hamilton on the thigh, and sits back.

PEGGY   What has my husband been accused of, Colonel Hamilton?

Hamilton hesitates. He wants to be sure that Arnold has no more to say, then:

HAMILTON   The first charge concerns the vessel *Charming Nancy*. It is claimed that you granted persons of disaffected character passes through our blockade.

ARNOLD   They asked for a pass—

HAMILTON (*Interrupting*)   Which enabled them to transport this ship out of British-occupied Philadelphia—

ARNOLD (*Interrupting*)   A pass to sneak a ship away from our enemies. What is wrong with that?!

HAMILTON (*Over this*)   Permitting a profit for these people. Their purpose was personal profit, sir!

ARNOLD   How did I know that?

Beat.

HAMILTON Profiteering, I have been asked to tell you, has become a crime promoted by Congress to a penalty of death. In some cases.

Beat.

ARNOLD I did not know these men. I did not know their plans. Perhaps I erred in judgment. Why is that a crime?

Beat.

HAMILTON Mr. Reed believes you had a financial interest in the *Charming Nancy*. Thus—you would be working for your own gain. Using your position—for profiteering.

Beat.

Reed has no proof. I can tell you this. But I have to ask you: Do you or did you have an interest in this vessel?

ARNOLD The *Charming Nancy*?

HAMILTON Yes.

ARNOLD Reed accuses me with no proof?

He covers his face and shakes his head—to show the burdens he must bear.

HAMILTON I take that to mean—no.

As he writes:

Excuse me.

Arnold turns to Peggy.

ARNOLD Schuyler's his new father-in-law.

She nods; she knows this.

(*He turns to Hamilton.*) I was *his* aide-de-camp, you know. As you are to—

109

HAMILTON (*Writing*) I know.

ARNOLD (*Looks to Hamilton, then to the women*) When Schuyler was interviewing me for the position, he put his big bearlike hand on my shoulder, and pointed about a hundred yards across a field to a big bright red barn. "Soldier!" he said in that warm voice he has.

This makes Hamilton smile, knowing how his father-in-law sounds.

"What color is that barn?" I look at the barn. I look at your father-in-law's face. I look back at the barn. "Any color you wish it to be, sir!" (*He bursts out laughing.*) I was hired on the spot.

Hamilton can't help but laugh a little, as well, though he continues to write.

Not an easy job, aide-de-camp. Not what people think. Is it?

Hamilton slightly shakes his head. Arnold sits back.

Good man, Schuyler. A goddamn crime what the politicians did to him.

HAMILTON (*Still writing*) He seems to bear no bitterness.

ARNOLD Get him drunk.

Short pause.

HAMILTON Second charge by—

PEGGY (*Interrupting*) Would you like more tea?

HAMILTON (*Shakes his head*) Second charge by Reed. Mr. Reed. That as you closed the shops in Philadelphia under martial law, as was your right and responsibility—

ARNOLD And my orders.

HAMILTON   Yes, that you continued to personally trade the goods of said shops—for profit—as well as committing extortion against those businesses you did close. War profiteering, I repeat, is a crime which now warrants hanging.

Short pause.

ARNOLD   As it should! So why not start with the fucking politicians? Hang 'em all, would be a good start. Reed first. The man was a failed shopkeeper before this war began. Did you know that? And he's a rich man now. How did that happen?

Turns to Peggy as he shakes his head in disgust. She holds his hand.

HAMILTON   If you could answer the charge—

ARNOLD   I was rich and now I've nothing. Nothing— material. (*He strokes Peggy's arm. To Hamilton*) When do I get to ask where my back pay and premiums are? I have detailed to the Congress what this great patriotic duty has cost me—I have lost ships, lands, my home. I am owed two thousand in pay. I have personally paid for blankets in Maine out of my own accounts.

HAMILTON   Send receipts.

ARNOLD   I've sent in the goddamn receipts! I have gained nothing from this war. It has taken my health. My fortune. I have made nothing. (*He sits back, suddenly tired, or he wants to show that he is tired.*) Pay me only what I'm owed, and let me go. I've had enough of this war. I have no more to give.

HAMILTON   You are a prized general in our army, sir. You must know the respect each soldier feels for you. And the honor all those feel for having served alongside you.

Arnold stares at Hamilton, then turns to Peggy.

ARNOLD (*Suddenly smiling*)   Hear that? (*He shakes his head, then on to another story.*) When those of us stupid enough to survive fell out of the great northern woods and onto the banks of the St. Lawrence—what we must have looked like. Half had no clothes. Their dicks frozen against their thighs. Keep walking, I said to them. Don't fight back. Don't question. We're good men. Fight a good fight. (*Beat*) I love my country, Colonel Hamilton.

HAMILTON   I didn't—

ARNOLD (*Over this*)   The country I knew—is in here. (*Touches his breast*) That helps—when I don't see it out there. I am innocent of the charge.

Short pause. Hamilton writes.

Again geese are heard overhead. Arnold struggles and stands—refusing help from Peggy. And with an imaginary rifle in hand, he pretends to shoot down a goose.

I hate cities.

HAMILTON (*Finishes writing*)   Third charge.

ARNOLD (*Interrupting*)   I like this boy. He does his job.

HAMILTON   Third—

ARNOLD   One minute. (*He struggles, perhaps too hard, to get back into his seat. Then he sits, leans over, and "gives all of his attention" to Hamilton.*)

HAMILTON   Third—charge. You've been accused of illegally using—commandeering—public wagons for personal business ventures. I believe there was a vessel you did have an interest in. We have those papers. And goods from this vessel were transported by public wagons? You've heard the charge before? Is this true?

ARNOLD Yes.

Short pause.

HAMILTON Is there anything you wish to add? An explanation?

Arnold picks up his cup, and Hannah pours him more coffee. When she finishes:

ARNOLD It is nowhere forbidden—to my knowledge—for one to engage in making money. Supporting one's family. Or is the complete ruination of my finances now a goal of Congress? And has fighting for your country now been promoted by goddamn politicians to a crime punishable by death?! (*Beat*) The ship you refer to is—a business enterprise. The goods transported from this vessel were goods—clothes, blankets, hides—much in need by our countrymen.

PEGGY (*To Hamilton*) People are going cold—

ARNOLD (*Over this*) And in transporting such goods I used public wagons that were not commandeered, as you call it, but, rather, sitting idle. And if you speak with the captain of these wagons—I'll give you his name—you will learn that I offered to pay for their use. A price determined not by me, but by the marketplace. What have I done wrong? (*Beat*) Colonel, what have I done that was wrong?

HAMILTON (*Writing*) I cannot answer—

ARNOLD When this country needed me, I was one of the first to give up all. Where were they? Where were my accusers? (*Beat*) But we are being naive. This—these attacks are not about me. The question is not what I have done wrong.

HAMILTON What are you—?

ARNOLD I'll tell you, son—I'm but a pawn in this. A piece on the board to knock over, to get to their catch—your general, sir, our commander in chief, General Washington!

HAMILTON I'm not sure that's—

ARNOLD They wish to replace him. Defeat him. They are afraid of his authority. They have Gates waiting in the wings. Someone they control—

HAMILTON (*Stops writing*) I won't take this down.

ARNOLD It's what this is about, boy! Open your eyes!

HAMILTON (*Over this*) You can't prove—

ARNOLD Don't you get it?

Peggy gets up and takes Arnold's hand. He calms down.

They are vile.

HAMILTON (*To Hannah*) I'll have some more of that tea, thank you.

HANNAH It's cold.

HAMILTON I'm thirsty, please.

She pours him more tea. Peggy has taken a handkerchief out of her husband's pocket and now wipes his face. Hamilton takes a deep breath, turns a page in his book and, before continuing, looks at Peggy.

ARNOLD What next? (*Realizes*) My wife?

HAMILTON A question. Not a specific accusation—

ARNOLD Because her father tried to choose the safety of his family over either side in this war? There is no shame in that! He's not a loyalist! He's a husband and father!

HAMILTON (*For the first time, stating his own opinion*) I don't agree with . . . (*Indicates the charge on the paper he holds*)

ARNOLD (*Over this*) And because my wife—(*Takes her hand*)—during the occupation happened to dance a few times with British soldiers? She told me about this! So she danced! She is a girl! Look at her! She meant no politics!

HAMILTON I agree, sir. I do agree with you on this—

ARNOLD (*Over this*) She meant to dance! Would your wife have been any different?

HAMILTON Probably not—

ARNOLD (*Over this*) I have not gone to war against seventeen-year-old girls!

HAMILTON Neither have I.

ARNOLD (*Over this*) Is it now a crime to wear an English dress? To listen to English music? Goddamnit, son—we speak English! For this I watched men die? For this I killed? For this I gave my leg?

HAMILTON (*At the same time*) No, no. No, sir.

ARNOLD If my marriage is my crime, then I am an unrepentant criminal!

HAMILTON It isn't, sir.

ARNOLD (*Over this*) Hang me, because I have a wife with taste! And grace! And beauty!

HAMILTON I can assure you, it isn't a crime. Please.

ARNOLD (*Over this*)   So hang me! Hang me, soldier!
Hang me!

Beat. They look at each other.

HAMILTON   As I said, I can see no crime there. Forgive me,
but I have to repeat everything. You understand, I am sure.

Arnold slowly nods, then suddenly slaps Hamilton on the back.

ARNOLD   I don't blame you, son.

HAMILTON   Thank you.

ARNOLD   You're a soldier. You do what you're told.

HANNAH   I'll get more tea. (*She stops, turns back. To Peggy*)
The musicians are here.

PEGGY   Show them inside.

Hannah hurries off.

Will you stay the night, Colonel?

HAMILTON   I've promised friends—

PEGGY   Then at least for dinner. (*She starts to go in.*) They play
as you eat. It helps the digestion. It's what they do in
England. (*She follows Hannah in.*)

HAMILTON   There are seven more charges, sir. Bear with me.
We'll get through them quickly, I'm sure.

SCENE FOUR

*The same, later that night. Inside the house, the musicians play.
Arnold sits alone, his leg propped up on a chair; he smokes a pipe.
After a moment, Hannah enters from the house, feigns a look at the
night sky, then:*

HANNAH They're dancing.

No response.

He's quite good. Polished. So is she. I hadn't seen Peggy dance before. She obviously enjoys it. Can I get you anything?

He shakes his head without looking at her.

They make quite a couple.

He looks at her.

Dancing. Ah—youth.

ARNOLD I'm not that old.

HANNAH I am. And I'm three years younger than you. (*She leans over conspiratorially.*) He already has a crush on her. I suppose your wife does that to men. (*He tries to ignore her.*) And he's just married himself. Can't be more than a month, is it? I think that's what he said. His wife is rich?

ARNOLD (*Puffs on his pipe*) Yes.

HANNAH So he's made a good match. (*Beat*) You know he was born a bastard.

ARNOLD (*Turning to her*) How would you know that—?

HANNAH (*Turning away*) The music's stopped. They've stopped. (*She listens.*) I never danced like that when I was young. When I was—no more than a child. Sometimes she looks no more than—

ARNOLD Hannah.

HANNAH She took Mr. Hamilton on a tour of the house.

ARNOLD Good.

HANNAH   She made it clear I wasn't to join them. Just her and him. They were gone about twenty minutes. (*Beat*) She's had three glasses of wine.

ARNOLD   Hannah, what are you now, a spy? Please let—

HANNAH (*Standing*)   If I'm in the way—

ARNOLD   I didn't mean—

HANNAH (*Over this*)   I worry about you—maybe I'm the only one who does. (*She turns to leave.*)

ARNOLD   I'm joking, come here! Sister, please! Come here.

Hannah stops, hesitates, then goes and takes Arnold's outstretched hand.

I appreciate . . . everything. You must know that. (*He reaches up and hugs her, kissing her on the forehead. She nearly melts.*) What would I ever do without you?

HANNAH (*Over this*)   You don't have to say—

ARNOLD   I mean it!

Peggy and Hamilton burst in from the house.

PEGGY (*Entering, heading for Arnold*)   Hannah, could you hand me that cushion? (*She goes and sits at Arnold's feet.*)

ARNOLD   Please, sit—there's a chair—

PEGGY   I wish to sit here.

Hannah hesitates, then gets the cushion and hands it to Peggy. During this:

HAMILTON   I have to say, General, you are a most lucky man. Your wife's beauty and charm surpass even her reputation.

PEGGY (*To Arnold*)   I thought he was a soldier, not a politician.

They smile.

HANNAH (*Giving Peggy the cushion*)   What reputation is that?

ARNOLD (*To Peggy*)   I think he's just an honest man.

HAMILTON   I was warned by General Washington to be on guard or I'd be swept off my feet by your wife. I will report that I have failed him.

Light laughter.

HANNAH   Just don't report it to your new wife.

Beat. Then they laugh at the "joke."

ARNOLD   He doesn't have a drink. We should get him a—

HAMILTON (*Over this*)   I've had more than enough. More than I should, thank you.

PEGGY (*Over this*)   Hannah, could you get the colonel a—

HAMILTON   I have to leave. I do.

Beat.

ARNOLD   I won't hear of—

HAMILTON   I must. (*Beat*) Please, don't make it any harder than it is. (*He shakes his head to sober up.*) My wife has relatives in Philadelphia. They expect me. (*He looks at his watch.*) My God—they've been expecting me. The new in-laws. I wouldn't wish to inconven—(*He has trouble saying the word, then tries again.*)—inconvenience them. Somehow I've gotten a little drunk. (*He wipes his face.*)

ARNOLD   That was our intention.

Hamilton, confused for a moment, looks at Arnold. Peggy suddenly laughs and slaps Arnold's arm.

PEGGY Benedict!

ARNOLD The cool air will clear your head. It's too stuffy inside.

Hamilton nods, hesitates, then:

HAMILTON I hope you're feeling better. (*He nods toward Arnold's raised leg.*)

ARNOLD I shouldn't have had the wine. I never learn.

Hamilton nods. He watches Arnold. Beat.

Is there anything . . . ?

HAMILTON I hope this afternoon was not too—painful. One does what one must.

ARNOLD I understand. Remember, I was secretary to your father-in-law.

This makes Hamilton laugh.

HAMILTON I really must . . .

ARNOLD Hannah will show you out. Good night.

Peggy, still at Arnold's feet, holds up her hand. Hamilton shakes it.

HAMILTON Good night. (*Then, staring at Arnold, blurting out*) I much admire you, sir. (*He turns and hurries out with Hannah.*)

Short pause.

From the house, the musicians begin another tune, but soon stop.

PEGGY (*Listening*) They don't know whether to play or not. There's no one in there.

ARNOLD What did you find out? Anything?

120

PEGGY (*Her head on his thigh*)   That General Washington has sided with you from the beginning. He's never believed the charges.

Arnold sits back and closes his eyes. Hannah returns carrying a small tray of glasses and liquor.

The fact that he has agreed to decide the matter personally is a very good thing. He knows what you've been going through. Such charges are even being circulated against him. They're being made against military governors in the South as well. (*Beat*) You are supported. These depositions—a formality.

ARNOLD   Then why put us through—?

PEGGY   They have no choice, he said. That boy is full of apologies.

Hannah sets the tray down.

HANNAH   Can you trust what he says? Are we sure—

PEGGY (*Ignoring her*)   And I'm sure he wished you to know all this. He just couldn't tell you himself, of course.

ARNOLD   So my responses this afternoon—

PEGGY   More than enough to address the charges. His recommendation to the general will be for complete exoneration. A recommendation the general shall accept with pleasure.

ARNOLD (*Relieved*)   Oh God.

PEGGY (*To Hannah*)   He told me all this while I showed him the house. You weren't there, were you?

ARNOLD   The nightmare of my life may be over. My honor, my self-respect—survives. I am an honest man. And I am a damn good soldier. (*He hugs Peggy, and nearly weeps with joy.*)

PEGGY He indicated that a request made now to return to a field command would be met with approval. They need you, Benedict.

ARNOLD It's where I can do some good.

He sits back. Hannah begins to pour him a drink.

No, I mustn't drink. I mustn't.

PEGGY Hannah, take away the tray. What could you be thinking?

HANNAH He always used to enjoy a drink before bed. I always got him a drink.

PEGGY (*Over this*) He can't anymore, Hannah. It inflames his leg.

ARNOLD (*Over this, reaching for the glass*) A little drink. A small one. It's been a good night. (*He takes a glass and sips.*)

Pause. Hannah sits and watches her brother. Both women are now staring at this man.

(*He sips and stares out.*) At Saratoga, Gates ordered me away from the lines. He took away my men. My horse. (*He looks at them.*) I've told you this a hundred times.

Both women shake their heads. "No, no, please."
"Tell me."

He'd taken everything from me—but my soul. I stole a horse. Disobeyed Gates. Charged to the line and led a charge that got so close to Bourgoyne I could see the blood rush out of his face. The powder off his wig on his shoulder. I just remembered that. Seven bullet holes in my hat, my coat. Fate protected me. As it protects me now. Damn it, I'm a soldier, and General Washington understands that. (*Beat*) He understands me. A good man. If it weren't for him . . . Like a father to me. (*Beat*) They say I looked crazed, deranged, as I charged. And that really scared them. Good. You have to do what you have to do. You pull it out of you from somewhere. (*Beat*) I gave my leg to my country. Now let me give it my life, if it wants it. Let me.

PEGGY (*Hugging Arnold*) I love you. It's a love greater than any I ever imagined possible. (*Beat*) My love for you grows greater and stronger each day, each hour and each minute. (*She turns to Hannah.*) Like our baby.

She touches her stomach. He kisses her head.

ARNOLD (*To Hannah*) Sister, would you please pay the musicians. It's late and there's no one dancing.

Hannah goes off. Arnold helps Peggy up and she sits on his lap.

PEGGY (*As she sits*) It doesn't hurt?

He kisses her. She sits back, and he takes out a letter and shows her.

ARNOLD Another from Andre. Or as he calls himself John Anderson. John Andre—John Anderson. He calls that a code. (*He smiles.*)

PEGGY I warned you he wasn't very bright. When he was here—he spent all of his time acting, putting on plays—

She stops; he has put the letter up to the candle flame.

ARNOLD Patience. A virtue I have long sought—without success. I should have just waited. I should never have written. (*Holding up the letter*) Do you mind? Will you be disappointed?

She shakes her head, and he burns the letter.

123

PEGGY I don't care where I live as long as it's with you. (*She hugs him, then touches her stomach.*) We'll go anywhere with you. Follow you—wherever. When I wake up, the first thought I have every day is that I am your wife, carrying your child. And I am so happy. I ask myself—what did I do to deserve such happiness?

They kiss.

If it's a boy, let's name him after the general, and call him George.

SCENE FIVE

New York City. A makeshift dressing room, backstage of the Theatre Royal, John Street. In the distance, a performance of Richard III *is going on.*
A British officer, Lieutenant-Colonel JOHN SIMCOE, *stands waiting, a file of papers to be signed in his hand.*
A noise off; he turns. Major Kemble enters, also with papers. They nod to each other, and wait. The performance continues off.

KEMBLE (*Finally*) You're waiting for Sir Henry as well.

SIMCOE I have papers for him to see.

Kemble shows his papers—he has papers for Sir Henry as well.

You knew where to find him.

KEMBLE Who doesn't?

Applause from the theatre.

SIMCOE Major Andre's in this, isn't he?

KEMBLE I believe so. A small role.

SIMCOE Is he as—talented—as they say?

KEMBLE I wouldn't know.

Andre, in costume (he plays a minor role in Richard III)*, enters with Sir Henry Clinton, who is in full uniform.*

SIR HENRY (*Entering*) I don't understand.

ANDRE You wanted to know who is sitting with Colonel Harvey, correct?

They notice Simcoe and Kemble. Andre goes to a table and sits and powders himself.

I'm telling you, Sir Henry, she is Delancy's wife.

SIR HENRY (*Caught up in the gossip*) But then where's Delancy?

ANDRE He's—well, what I've been told is—in essence—he's loaned her to Colonel Harvey.

SIR HENRY I truly don't understand. You can't mean—

ANDRE And Colonel Harvey—for this pleasure—has made Delancy the sole supplier for the army. So Delancy's getting rich.

SIR HENRY Unbelievable. (*To Simcoe and Kemble*) I can't fathom—(*He turns back to Andre.*) Off his wife's hole? (*He stands incredulous. Then, seeing the papers:*) Are those for me? (*He takes them and skims.*)

ANDRE Would you like to meet her? She'd probably like to meet you.

SIR HENRY I don't think—(*He turns to Kemble and laughs.*) No, I don't think I would at all. Can you believe that? The man rents his wife. Americans! I don't know why I let them surprise me anymore! Are you watching? John's terribly good tonight. Let me do that. You've missed a whole spot.

Sir Henry goes and powders Andre. Kemble stands and watches.

KEMBLE I'm sure the major is a very fine actor. (*Beat*) The theatre's not my pleasure, I'm afraid.

SIR HENRY Neither was it mine until I saw John.

SIMCOE (*Going through his papers*) If that will be all?

Andre has unbuttoned his tunic.

ANDRE I'm sweating through this.

SIR HENRY Let me. (*He begins to powder Andre's bare chest.*)

Simcoe looks at Kemble and leaves. Kemble hesitates, then turns back.

KEMBLE Oh Major—any reply from "Monk"?

Beat. Andre looks at Sir Henry, then responds.

ANDRE Not yet. I expect—anytime now.

KEMBLE I'm sure—you're in control of things.

SIR HENRY We need patience. We just need to wait. John understands that. Washington's favorite general? A big fish. And they take the most time.

Kemble goes, as the STAGE MANAGER *enters.*

STAGE MANAGER Your cue is coming, Major. (*Leaves*)

ANDRE Thank you, Sir Henry. That will do fine. It's only a minor role. (*He laughs lightly and begins to exit.*)

SIR HENRY I'll come and watch again from the wings. If that's all right. I enjoy that terribly.

They go.

Morristown, New Jersey. Washington's headquarters. A private room at Dickerson's Tavern. A small table and a few chairs.
Empty. Arnold, in full dress, walks in. He looks around.
Hamilton enters from another door.

HAMILTON General Arnold. I just heard you'd arrived. You're a few minutes early. His Excellency will be with you shortly.

ARNOLD Tell him to take his time. (*He smiles.*) I'm in no rush.

Hamilton sets a folder on the table.

How are you, Colonel? And how's your bride?

HAMILTON I've hardly seen her for two months, sir. Would you like something to drink?

Arnold shrugs.

I'll get something for you. His Excellency isn't drinking.

ARNOLD Then don't bother, I won't—

HAMILTON (*Leaving*) He'll insist.

After a beat, GENERAL GEORGE WASHINGTON, forty-seven, enters. He looks exhausted. When he sees Arnold he lights up.

WASHINGTON My God—it's a soldier! How the hell did you get past all those politicians?

Arnold smiles.

ARNOLD Just pushed my way through, sir. Shot a few along the way. I hope you don't mind.

WASHINGTON Here—take a medal.

Hamilton enters.

HAMILTON Are we feeding them or not?

Arnold doesn't know what he's talking about.

WASHINGTON (*To Hamilton*) No one offered to pay?

Hamilton shakes his head.

Unbelievable.

ARNOLD (*To Hamilton*) What's—?

HAMILTON A delegation from Congress. I've put them in the next room.

ARNOLD And they expect the army to feed them—?

WASHINGTON (*Over this*) There's one a week now. Except when it rains.

HAMILTON Or cold.

WASHINGTON I can't wait for winter. They leave you alone then.

HAMILTON They've ordered food.

WASHINGTON Get the tavern keep to write out a bill. Put it in front of them. Point. These are not poor men.

Hamilton goes. Washington's mind drifts for a moment, then:

Mr. Arnold, it is very good to see you. I ordered us lunch. You want to drink something—?

ARNOLD Colonel Hamilton—

WASHINGTON He won't bring the wine. He's hoarding the wine. It'll be rum.

ARNOLD I don't mind.

WASHINGTON In Philadelphia is there wine?

ARNOLD It can be found.

WASHINGTON They say you live well in Philadelphia.

ARNOLD In general? Or me personally?

WASHINGTON You, sir. What I've heard is about you.

Beat.

ARNOLD I am the military governor of the city. I am a general in the United States Army. I live no better nor worse than I must and should.

Beat.

WASHINGTON Why the hell didn't I say that? They were into my books just last month. Where's the receipt for this? Where's the receipt for that? I try to say when you lift a squealing pig off a Tory farm, it isn't too likely you'll get a receipt. What war are they fighting? I don't know. (*Beat*) You must feel the same way.

ARNOLD Yes sir, I do.

WASHINGTON They want your scalp. (*Beat*) And they want mine.

ARNOLD Do they?

Short pause.

WASHINGTON Well, we're not here to talk about me. Mr. Adams has proposed in Congress that all generals should be elected. I wrote and said, great. I vote for Mr. Adams to be on the front lines. (*Beat*) He withdrew his proposal. They don't know what they are doing. And they're bringing us all down with them. Tell me, what is the currency rate on the street? No one will tell me.

Beat.

ARNOLD I believe it's five hundred U.S. paper dollars to one guinea. But that was yesterday—it's probably worse now.

Pause.

WASHINGTON I tell them, get someone else. I'm not a military genius. Get Gates. He wants it bad. Look what he did to Schuyler. Just because the man disagreed with him. No one wants to discuss anything anymore. Everyone's screaming at everyone. Who's the real American? And they're all just such goddamn hypocrites! Your Mr. Reed, your accuser—he's trying to bring God into this now. What the hell does God have to do with a war? If he'd been with us this winter— he'd have had to conclude that if he wanted to be on God's side, it wasn't ours. (*Short pause*) There was a moment last winter—Hamilton knocked on my cabin. Twenty men— enlisted—wanted to see me. More desertion. More failure. They come in. I just look into the fire, waiting for them to begin to justify—their families. Their farms. They're hungry. Who gives a shit, they're soldiers! But . . . (*He shrugs.*) Then, one begins to speak, a young boy really—how they have come to enlist again—for another year. In the midst of a blizzard. They had no shoes, Benedict. I looked at them. In the firelight. Their eyes red from sickness. Their clothes torn and bloody. And I went to each one . . . (*He begins to cry.*) And I hugged them. I held them. I told them how proud of them I . . . (*He can't go on for a moment.*)

Hamilton comes in with rum, glasses, and food. As he sets these down on the table, he and Arnold exchange glances.

130

Washington wipes the tears, pours himself a glass of rum.

Rum. What did I tell you? (*He drinks.*)

Hamilton sits down at a distance.

Are you broke too?

Short pause.

ARNOLD I can't sell my house in New Haven.

WASHINGTON Who'd buy it? And for what—our worthless paper money? I've started to burn it for heat. Wipe myself with it. Sometimes you feel like an utter fool. Everyone's getting rich. Everyone I know it seems.

Hamilton stirs in his chair.

Is that what this was really about—money? (*Beat*) Makes you want to curse—the whole species, Mr. Arnold. It can't just be an American trait, Benedict. It must be everyone. Somehow that gives some comfort.

Hamilton comes over and cuts the meat for Washington.

(*In pain, with his eyes closed*) Dr. Rush has written an anonymous letter to Patrick Henry, calling me incompetent. (*Beat*) Anonymous. I recognized the handwriting. I have spies too. (*Beat*) Dr. Rush is a very good and close friend of mine. (*Short pause. He drinks, turns to Hamilton.*)

HAMILTON The delegation will see you whenever you're ready.

WASHINGTON (*To Arnold*) How's your beautiful young wife?

ARNOLD She's—

WASHINGTON I hear she's pregnant. Good for you. Have children, then you don't have to feel you must do

everything yourself. In your life. A man's greatest mistake—
not to have a child. I speak from experience. (*Beat. He
suddenly smiles.*) Also a damn good excuse to make yourself a
little money—"for the family." Who argues with that?

*Washington is more and more into himself. Arnold sits and watches
this man who is in so much pain.*

Do you dream, sir?

ARNOLD I do. But I can never recall what I've dreamed.

*A knock on the door (off). Hamilton gets up and goes to the door
(off), exiting.*

WASHINGTON (*As he picks at his food*) Martha tells me I sit up
and scream in the night. I don't recall either. I just
remember how painful it was. I try to avoid sleep now. But
that's not good, is it? God knows when I've slept last. (*Beat*)
They say we must end the war by next summer. (*Beat*)
Impossible. (*Beat*) But then we run out of money. Bullshit.
(*Pause*) It is good to talk to a soldier.

Hamilton returns.

HAMILTON They'd like to see you now.

WASHINGTON They'd like to see me. (*He pours himself more
rum. To Arnold*) About a month ago, I was offered an
earldom. From the king. What do they take me for? They
were going to throw in—the name of a city. My name.
Washington. The name of a city. My choice. Philadelphia?
Even Boston. I said who the hell wants a city named after
him? They don't understand. Sometimes I fear in my
deepest soul that no one understands. That I'm fighting this
goddamn war for reasons that are perverse and
contradictory. That I'm a pawn for speculators, embezzlers,

stockjobbers and a whole sea of monstrous intentions. But in my soul, we fight for principle. Or am I alone? (*Beat*) Do you ever feel like that, Benedict?

No response.

Look at what they've given me to get you to sign. Why no one else would do it, I don't know. There. (*He hands him a piece of paper.*) It's a loyalty oath. We're all signing them now. I signed mine last week. Ask me how humiliated *I* felt.

ARNOLD Why a loyalty—?

WASHINGTON Because they don't have anything else to think about! And they sit in their mansions, refusing to pay money for this war, and wonder why the hell does a man like Washington put up with us at all? Someday it's going to dawn on him just what a sucker he's been, so we better get him to sign a loyalty oath. So I signed. So sign. (*Beat*) Sign.

Arnold hesitates, then signs his name. Hamilton takes the oath away. Pause; Washington looks into Arnold's face.

HAMILTON Sir, they're waiting.

WASHINGTON (*To Arnold*) Do you believe in God, Benedict?

ARNOLD (*Stunned by the question*) I—I don't know what to—I pray—!

WASHINGTON (*Over this*) I don't mean a *good* God, or even one with a *heaven* where nice folk go, or to the *devil* where the bad go. I'm not saying any particular kind of God. Just—God. (*Beat*) Knowable or unknowable. Is there a God? Mr. Hamilton thinks there isn't.

Arnold looks to Hamilton.

And he has just about convinced me.

Washington stands, as does Arnold. Washington opens the folder and takes out a paper.

Now, my apologies for this formality, but it's what I agreed to do. Let me read to you my rebuke.

ARNOLD Your what? I'm sorry?

WASHINGTON I've had to find you guilty of two of the charges.

Arnold is in shock.

(*He reads.*) "The commander in chief would have been much happier in an occasion of bestowing commendations on an officer who has rendered such distinguished services to his country as Major General Arnold; but in the present case, a sense of duty and a regard to candor oblige him to declare that he considers his conduct in the instance of the permit as peculiarly reprehensible, both in civil and military views, and in the affair of the wagons as imprudent and improper." (*He closes the folder.*) There. That's done. I hope they do replace me with Gates. Let's see him deal with this crap.

ARNOLD I don't understand, Your Excellency. I'm innocent.

WASHINGTON No doubt.

Arnold, confused, to each man.

ARNOLD I've done nothing wrong.

Washington looks away; Hamilton steps forward.

HAMILTON The Committee of Pennsylvania threatened to withdraw support—wagons, supplies—from the army unless you were punished. We had no choice.

ARNOLD That's bullshit! This is my honor!

HAMILTON You're the butt of gossip. Of talk. You've lost the confidence of the people of Philadelphia. (*He tries to hand Arnold a piece of paper—his orders.*) You're relieved of your duty as governor there. We understand you'd be interested in a field commission. Or command of a fleet?

WASHINGTON (*Half to himself*) What fleet? (*He laughs*)

HAMILTON And can you ride a horse yet? (*Beat*) We are assigning you to command the fort at West Point.

WASHINGTON It's a mess. You fix it.

HAMILTON Sir, you have the appearance of scandal around you. We had no choice.

ARNOLD Cowards.

HAMILTON (*Getting upset*) You don't speak to His Excellency like that—!

WASHINGTON (*Over this*) We compromised. They wanted you in jail.

ARNOLD It's not me they want. You know that yourself—

WASHINGTON Of course not.

HAMILTON But we couldn't let them get to the general, could we?

WASHINGTON I will make this up to you. You have my promise.

He holds out his hand. Arnold doesn't take it.

ARNOLD You betrayed me.

WASHINGTON That's one opinion. Mine is that outside this tavern are twelve thousand men waiting for blankets, food,

135

pay. It's them I must not betray. (*Beat*) You are acting far too upset. It's a piece of paper. You still have my confidence.

ARNOLD   Then say that! Write that down!

HAMILTON   He can't.

ARNOLD (*Over this*)   Just tell that delegation!

Washington holds out his hands—gesturing that there is nothing he can do. Arnold bolts from the table.

WASHINGTON (*To Hamilton*)   Let the bastards wait. That's what I do every day. Maybe one of them will get the hint and pay their bill. (*He tries to smile.*) General, sit down and have another drink.

Washington pours. Arnold stays at a distance.

How's the wife? A beautiful woman, isn't she, Colonel?

HAMILTON   I'm in love with her myself.

WASHINGTON (*Pouring; to Hamilton*)   You told me you danced with her?

HAMILTON (*Accepting a glass*)   The high point of my visit to Philadelphia.

WASHINGTON (*Drinking*)   He's a lucky man. (*Beat*) And she's expecting. Good for you. (*He turns to Hamilton.*) How come yours isn't pregnant yet?

HAMILTON   Sir, I've hardly been allowed home since—

WASHINGTON (*Winking at Arnold and laughing*)   Excuses! The boy makes excuses! I wouldn't! We wouldn't. (*He laughs.*) But these young ones . . . Look at him, Benedict. (*He "presents" Hamilton to Arnold.*) The boy still thinks the world will wait for him.

Washington smiles at Arnold, then patronizingly takes Hamilton's hand and pats it.

But we know better, General, don't we. It won't. (*He puts down his glass and straightens his coat.*) I suppose I've put it off as long as I can. Politicians. (*He shakes his head. He looks at Arnold, who stares at him.*) My regards, General, to your beautiful young wife.

Washington goes. Short pause.

HAMILTON Don't do anything you'll regret. (*Beat*) He loves us like sons. So think of his pain. Accept West Point. There are worse places. (*He turns to go, stops.*) There's a guard posted outside their room. (*He nods toward where Washington exited.*) When His Excellency meets with members of Congress, they don't wish to be disturbed. (*Beat*) Go home. Your horse is outside. Saddled.

ARNOLD I didn't ask—

HAMILTON I did. I thought you'd wish to leave—quickly.

Hamilton leaves.

SCENE SEVEN

Philadelphia; the Penn Mansion, sitting room.
    Arnold enters, his coat dusty from the road. (He has just arrived back from Morristown.) He begins to take off his coat. Hannah, in a nightgown, arrives, candle in hand.

HANNAH What are you doing back? I thought you weren't coming home until—

ARNOLD (*Still removing his coat*) Get me something to eat.

Hannah hesitates.

Please, Hannah. I haven't eaten.

Hannah hurries off. Arnold gets his coat off and flings it on the ground. He throws himself into the chair and begins to try and take his boots off. This clearly is causing him both pain and frustration.
Hannah enters with a tray just as he finally gets a boot off and flings it across the room.
She brings him the tray. He begins to eat. She watches.

HANNAH You must be tired. It's so late. I couldn't sleep myself. (*She looks at him for a moment.*) I'm not sure this is the right time, but I would like to raise something with you. It's been on my mind all day. It's why I couldn't— sleep.

He eats.

While I was in one of the shops today, Mrs.—you don't know her—a friend of mine, she asks how Peggy is doing.

Arnold looks up at her as he continues to eat.

I say, what do you mean? She—Peggy's—perfectly fine. And then she says, I mean with the pregnancy. It's often the first two months that are the most difficult. She says this as if I'd never heard it. As if I couldn't know. Well, Benedict, I was told by you—and Peggy—ordered—that this "situation"—Peggy's, it was to be kept private. So I've said nothing. And there are many people I would have liked to have told. (*Beat*) So is it private or not? I've told no one.

ARNOLD (*Incredulous*) Hannah—

HANNAH I will admit, Benedict, to feeling hurt. When I heard—it was like she thought *I* didn't know. You can imagine the position that puts me in—

Arnold suddenly can't take it anymore; the frustration mounting from his talk with Washington erupts at Hannah.

138

ARNOLD Goddamnit woman, stop it! Will you be quiet! I can't take your stupidity anymore! Stop! Stop!

Hannah bursts out crying, and moves away. Peggy enters in a nightgown.

PEGGY What's—? Benedict, when did you—? Hannah? What happened? Hannah?

She goes to Hannah, who pushes her away and runs out of the room. Peggy looks at her husband. Pause.

Hannah can be heard crying—off.

ARNOLD I've been found guilty of two crimes. By General Washington.

PEGGY How can . . . ? (*She stops herself.*)

ARNOLD And I've been censured. And sent away.

PEGGY That's not possible.

ARNOLD It feels like they've rammed a hand down my throat and reamed my soul.

PEGGY There's been a mistake. You've misunderstood.

ARNOLD (*Over this*) He traded me for wagons! (*He takes out a very crumpled newspaper.*) His published verdict.

Peggy takes it and begins to read. Hannah slowly returns at a distance.

PEGGY (*As she reads*) I don't believe this.

Hannah cautiously approaches with a letter in hand. She sniffles hard, trying not to cry.

ARNOLD Hannah, I didn't mean—

HANNAH This just came.

He takes the letter.

PEGGY   At this hour?

Arnold tries to pull Hannah toward him.

ARNOLD   Hannah . . . (*He tries to kiss her on the cheek.*) I didn't
mean—of course, it must have been awful for you, hearing
that woman talk about—our baby. (*The "our," he makes clear,
refers to the three of them.*) But things get out. So forgive me.
(*He turns back to Peggy.*) There's more: I've been made
commander of the fort at West Point. On the Hudson.

PEGGY   Why would—?

ARNOLD   I'm out of the way there, I suppose.

HANNAH   I don't think we should leave—

ARNOLD (*Yells*)   We have to! (*He then quickly grabs her hand, to
keep her from crying.*) There is no choice.

Pause. Peggy finishes reading the verdict and sets it down.

(*To no one*) All the way back, I kept listing the battles I have
fought in.

PEGGY   And I thought Washington was your—

ARNOLD   He's not. (*Short pause*) It's beautiful country.
Around West Point. Dramatic. (*He smiles*) Memorable. I
was thinking, on our way up there we could detour a little,
reach the Hudson say at Tappan and follow the river from
there? I wouldn't mind seeing it all again—one more time.
As I remember, it changes just about every mile.

PEGGY   You know it well then—?

ARNOLD   I've been up and down that river more times than I
can count.

Peggy goes and comforts Hannah. She hugs her.

First—at Haverstraw Bay—you'd think you were on the
edge of a sea. It's vast, more lake than river, with green
tumbling hills, dipping into the river's shore. As idyllic a
picture as one can imagine, I would think. (*Beat*) Then
there's a sudden twist, and the river narrows ten times, and
this lake becomes a twisting river of force; it cuts through
mountains on one side, farms on the other. The Wild
West—divided from the settled earth. It's how it feels.

Hannah continues to cry.

And then another sudden turn, and it's a gorge you're in
now. Steep slopes, cliffs, and there before you—on the
west side, is West Point. With its forts, buildings, old
walls, as but the foreground for the glorious Catskills
behind. Huge peaks of nature, nature untouched by
people—pristine, raw and free. Uncompromised earth.
(*Beat*) Were I to ever leave—

Peggy turns when she hears this.

—it is what I would miss of my country. Such beauty. Such
places. (*Beat*) You'll see. We'll detour.

Peggy moves from Hannah and approaches Arnold.

PEGGY Were *we* to ever leave . . . (*She takes his hand, then
looks off.*) Though sometimes it feels like we've already left.
Or what we had—is gone. Last spring at the Meschianza
Ball? I've told you about—by the way, that's where I first
met John Andre.

He looks at her.

Remember him?

HANNAH   Who's John Andre?

PEGGY   The dress I wore was made of silk. A pale green, and it flowed—like an animal running over a hill, that smoothly. The dressmaker was such a success. I'm told the style was the latest in London. I felt I was the belle of the ball.

HANNAH   Who's John—

ARNOLD   A major. British.

Hannah starts to say something, but Peggy interrupts.

PEGGY   (*To Arnold*)   It was actually more than a ball. More like being inside a fairy tale. With knights and princesses. My friend Peggy Chew was saying the other day that she was dying to put on a play. Just for fun. What harm could that be? (*Beat*) But plays are forbidden here. Why?

He looks at her, then turns away.

ARNOLD   I don't know.

She waits to see if he has more to say, then continues.

PEGGY   In New York City they are still doing plays. Having concerts. *They* haven't closed anything. But then of course—that's the British influence. Culture. (*She remembers suddenly.*) My dressmaker for the ball? She's dead. Starved to death, I think.

Arnold has been fiddling with the letter in his hand. Peggy suddenly takes it, opens it, and quickly reads the few lines.

From Reed. And the committee. They've seen the verdict. (*She hands the letter back to her husband.*) We're to vacate this house by noon tomorrow.

HANNAH   Tomorrow? We can't possibly—!

PEGGY (*Over this, to Arnold*)   We have to leave by tomorrow! He says you were fortunate to have got off so easy.

Arnold still doesn't look at the letter.

But he got what he wanted. (*To Hannah*) And we'll take only one trunk. And we'll carry it out the front door ourselves. Let them see how little we possess. What little he has left!

Short pause. They say nothing. The candle flickers, and suddenly Peggy grabs her stomach, flinching.

ARNOLD (*Taking her hand*)   What? You feel the baby? Is it kicking?

PEGGY (*Shaking her head*)   I think it's too soon for that. (*To Hannah*) Is it?

HANNAH   I don't know.

Short pause.

PEGGY   I saw a man on the street yesterday, who was getting money from people for farting in such a way that it almost sounded like "God Save the King." I couldn't watch. What a country. (*Beat. She rubs her stomach.*) Peggy Chew says that hundreds and hundreds of books—(*She takes Arnold's hand and rubs it across her stomach.*)—aren't even sent to America. Because nobody reads here.

ARNOLD (*Pulling his hand back*)   That isn't true!

She looks at him.

PEGGY   Hardly anyone.

Pause.

ARNOLD   Maybe.

She takes his hand and holds it in hers.

PEGGY Father says nearly everyone's started going back to church. They feel they have to. He says they're afraid if they're not seen in church things will be said about them. (*Beat*) So loving your country isn't enough anymore, Father says. Now you have to love your country's God. (*Beat*) People are afraid to say what they really think. That's what Father says. People are scared.

Short pause.

SCENE EIGHT

Months later. Haverstraw, five miles south of West Point. A field overlooking the Hudson River. Night. Howling wind.

ANDRE (*Off*) Mr. Monk? Is that you?

Andre, out of uniform, enters, holding up a lantern.

Sir?

Arnold enters from the opposite direction. Short pause.

ARNOLD Mr.—Anderson?

They look at each other for a moment. Andre hears something and turns to where Arnold entered.

ANDRE Who's that?

ARNOLD My orderly. He'll keep his distance.

ANDRE Wouldn't it be best to . . .

ARNOLD (*Turns, and calls*) Sergeant, stay with the horses! (*Back to Andre*) Why aren't you in uniform?

ANDRE (*Ignoring him, looking off*) What a thrilling night. Is it not? One could not imagine anything more dramatic.

ARNOLD It's an area I'm very fond of—the Hudson.

ANDRE I've journeyed up it myself. Soon after I arrived in this country. To Quebec. To fight you, General.

Arnold looks at him.

I'm a great fan of yours. You've been quite the thorn in the side. I admire that. Soldier to soldier.

ARNOLD (*Looks toward the Hudson*) Your ship, *The Vulture*— it's staying too close. My men will shell it. It should move off and come back—for the pickup.

ANDRE Perhaps we should go now then. While it's there. You've brought nothing with you? (*Beat*) Or are you still unsure?

ARNOLD (*Suddenly*) How committed are you British to winning this war?

ANDRE Sir, I can promise—

ARNOLD (*Over this*) Do you have the stomach for it? I have wondered that often enough. Your army sits in New York—

ANDRE Sir Henry believes patience—

ARNOLD I need to know the depth of your passion! I need to know if you *believe*! And that you will act justly and honorably upon your beliefs! (*Beat*) Have I made myself clear?

Beat.

ANDRE I can assure you, sir, that as long as there's an England, these colonies will be *of* that England. You have my word. Sir Henry Clinton is as committed to this cause as he is to his own life. And I, sir, am willing to suffer a painful death for its noble sake.

Short pause. Arnold says nothing.

Should we go?

There is no response.

We haven't talked compensation.

Arnold turns to hear this.

For such a brave act as this, my government expects to pay— something. Out of gratitude. Having you on our side will do much for morale, for one thing. What are you seeking?

ARNOLD (*After some hesitation*) I wish only to be given what I'm already owed by Congress, both in back pay and loans made. (*Beat*) And—for the value of my property in New Haven, which shall surely be confiscated when my actions here become known. (*He looks at Andre.*)

ANDRE Do you have a figure amount?

ARNOLD In pounds?

ANDRE What else is there?

Beat.

ARNOLD Ten thousand. And this constitutes no profit on my behalf. Only reimbursement—

ANDRE I understand—

ARNOLD And pay for what I'm giving up. My claim's now in—I do not wish to end up indigent in my—

146

ANDRE I understand. And what you ask seems fair—

ARNOLD (*Over this*) I am no Judas. This is not how I see myself, nor how I wish to be seen. I do not do this for money! It is my hope that my actions here will give courage to others to do the same. And if I accept no more than what I'm owed, then the virtue of what I do can't be questioned. It will be seen that I act in good conscience, honor intact, and for what is in the best interest of my country.

Beat.

ANDRE I salute you. It is indeed a noble thing you do. I am in a position to guarantee the request.

Andre looks to Arnold, expecting him to go with him now, but Arnold hesitates, then sits on the ground.
Andre takes out a flask.

Would you like a . . . ? (*He notices that the flask is nearly empty.*) I have another.

He takes out another, offers it to Arnold, who ignores it. Then Andre takes a big swig himself. In fact, it slowly becomes clear that Andre is a bit drunk already.
Andre, to be friendly, sits on the ground as well.

(*After a pause*) Beautiful night. How is your lovely wife? I assume she must be . . . ? She'll be joining you, I assume.

ARNOLD She's fine. (*Beat. For a moment he is lost in thought.*) She says you're a—poet?

ANDRE (*Smiling*) I've written—

ARNOLD (*Over this*) And actor. She talks about a ball, when you were in Philadelphia.

ANDRE (*Over this*) The Meschianza.

ARNOLD I can never understand what she's—it sounds so—it doesn't make sense.

ANDRE (*Over the end of this*) A little something to keep the men's spirits up. A festival really. To celebrate General Howe's return to London. (*Beat*) I created a tilt and tournament, like those of the ancient knights. We had armor; I was in charge of the hats myself. I could step into the life of a milliner now. Should one want that. (*Beat*) We had jousts. The ladies dressed in Turkish costume. Your wife was adorable. It was fun. Everyone in Philadelphia had fun. Everyone invited. It cost a fortune. (*He laughs.*) It was like a play, but without an audience, only actors. The Knights of the Blended Rose. Their motto: "We droop when separated." (*He laughs and drinks.*) The Knights of the Burning Mountain. Their motto: "I burn forever." (*He smiles.*) We redid a whole mansion. You walk in and it's like—hundreds of years ago. It got us through the winter. The general was very pleased.

Beat.

ARNOLD My wife had a good time.

ANDRE My greatest achievement in America—so far. It's why I'm a major. Caused a hell of a lot of resentment—my promotion. But this—(*Gestures toward Arnold*)—will change everything for me. (*Beat*) Sir, I think we should go.

ARNOLD I am not coming with you today, Major Andre.

ANDRE (*Suddenly standing and angry*) Then what am I doing here? Why did you insist that I come? I do not enjoy wasting my time—

ARNOLD I asked you to come—(*He gets Andre's attention.*)— so that I could offer you not only myself, but my command,

148

the three forts at West Point, and its three thousand eighty-six men. They are yours.

Andre is stunned. After a pause.

ANDRE And how is such an offer—to be accepted? Will you march them down the river—

ARNOLD (*Takes maps and papers out of his coat*) A tally of my army's strength, maps of the forts, with locations of weakness marked. A copy of the plan in event of alarm, again with weaknesses indicated. A proposed attack plan, including strength needed, types of equipment and so forth. You will see that, as presently organized, West Point stands completely vulnerable, to even the most modest assault. And with myself in charge of the defenders, there can be no chance of failure. (*He holds out maps and papers to Andre.*) It's now clear why I insisted that we meet?

ANDRE (*Walking around, excited*) My God, they'll make me a bloody general. And they laugh at me now. I know they do. (*To Arnold*) I came to this godforsaken country because—I was a bloody clerk at home. They wouldn't even let me become an actor! So I'm here. Three thousand men! (*He opens the flask. Offering*) Please . . .

ARNOLD I'm not finished. (*Beat*) This assault must be taken tomorrow night. For good reason. This morning, in a few hours, a guest will arrive in my house. I shall spend the day with him, showing him the weakness of our fortifications. This will disappoint him, but not make him suspicious. Because he visits in part to make amends for errors made toward me. (*Beat*) I will forgive him. Embrace him. And he will spend the night. (*Beat*) He is General George Washington. Commander in chief of our army. With the capture of West Point, you capture him. (*Beat*) A good

149

man. He's supported me throughout my political troubles, coming to my aid again and again. There have been times, when I saw him as my father. (*Short pause*) You achieve this, Major, and the war is over.

Silence. The wind. Then birds are heard overhead. Arnold looks up.

They should be asleep.

Cannon fire is heard off.

ANDRE What's that?

ARNOLD My men are firing on your ship. You'd better signal to be picked up. I dare not order them to stop.

More cannon fire. Andre takes a swig from his flask.
Arnold watches where the cannon shot hits in the river.

They're close. Your ship can't send a launch now.

ANDRE What am I going—?

ARNOLD (*Over this*) I'll get a couple of men from the battery to row you over. I'll tell them—you're taking messages from me.

Andre takes another swig.

Just signal for them not to leave!

ANDRE General. You are the first true American patriot.

ARNOLD Don't kiss my ass, Major. I've never found that pleasant. And do stop drinking. (*He looks at him.*) My God, have I made a mistake?'

ANDRE You haven't, sir. I give you my word. And I am sober. (*He takes the flask and throws it into the woods.*) Good day, sir. And good fortune.

ARNOLD   Hide those papers. And signal!

Arnold hurries off.

  Cannon fire continues. Andre holds the papers, wonders where to hide them. He takes off his boot and stuffs them in. Then, with the lantern, he stands signaling the boat, using the lamp's shutter.

  More cannon fire; voices shouting are heard in the near distance. Andre hears them, turns to them.

ANDRE   Here! I'm here!

TWO SKINNERS (*half soldier/half highwayman*) *enter and stop when they see the smiling Andre.*

  Andre turns and sees a signal from the ship.

  They'll stay where they are. But we should go. Where's the boat?

Beat.

PAULING   What boat?

VAN WART (*Looking off*)   Why's she staying put? She's still in range. Is she firing back? (*To Andre*) Who are you?

ANDRE   Weren't you sent by General—

PAULING   No one sent us.

VAN WART (*Over this*)   Who are you?

ANDRE (*Realizing*)   Oh God. Where's—? (*He looks for Arnold's men.*) My name is Anderson. John Anderson. Merchant. I have a pass. (*He begins to look in his jacket.*) From your commanding officer, General Arnold—

VAN WART   We're local. Private soldiers.

ANDRE (*Panicking*)   I need to go, please.

They stop him.

My God, I must get along! I'm doing the general's business!

PAULING   Look at them boots. Them are British soldier boots.

ANDRE   I bought "them" in New York. That's all they sell. What do you want? I have a pass! (*He takes out a paper.*) Will you look at it?

VAN WART   What are you doing out here at night?

ANDRE   Damn it, man, read it! What do you want? You want to rob me? Here—it's all I have. (*He hands him his purse.*)

VAN WART   British money.

ANDRE   I live in New York! Of course I have—it's real money. If you want more—give me your names. I'll send some—or on my next trip to West Point—

PAULING   Give me your boots. Look at my boots. I need boots.

ANDRE (*Over this*)   I can't give you my boots! What else? Here, take my cloak. It's wool.

VAN WART (*Suddenly hits him across the face*)   Give Mr. Pauling your boots!

Andre falls down, bleeding from the mouth. Pauling takes off Andre's boots.

(*To Pauling*) Give me his cloak! I need his cloak!

Andre watches as Pauling finds the papers in the boot.

PAULING (*To Van Wart*)   What's this?

Andre suddenly runs off in his bare feet.

VAN WART Hey, you bastard! Get back here! Get him!

The two Skinners run off in pursuit.

> *After a moment Arnold's two SOLDIERS enter with a lantern. They look around.*

SOLDIER Mr. Anderson? (*He calls.*) Mr. Anderson?

They go off.

> (*Off*) Mr. Anderson? Mr. Anderson?

SCENE NINE

West Point. A room in Arnold's house overlooking the Hudson River. Table, a few chairs. Night. Cannon fire continues in the distance.

> *Arnold enters, sweating and tired (he has just returned from his meeting with Andre). Hannah follows him, lighting a lamp. Arnold sits, then turns, hearing voices off.*

ARNOLD Who's that? Peggy?

Hannah nods and sets the lamp on the table.

> She's still up? (*He listens.*) Who's she with? Who's she talking to?

HANNAH Colonel Hamilton. He arrived a few hours ago, to prepare for His Excellency's visit.

Short pause.

ARNOLD Tell my wife I'm here.

HANNAH I wouldn't want to disturb them. They sound like they're—enjoying themselves.

ARNOLD (*Over the end of this*) Tell her, Hannah.

Hannah goes off. Voices. Arnold takes out a pipe and fills it. Peggy, very pregnant now, enters with Hamilton. Hannah follows. Peggy and Hamilton both carry glasses.

PEGGY You're back. (*She goes to kiss him.*)

HAMILTON (*At the same time*) General, how are you?

ARNOLD (*At the same time; trying to stand*) Colonel, I didn't expect you tonight—

HAMILTON (*Over this*) Don't get up.

An awkward moment; no one knows what to say.

(*Finally*) Being in the country has done you a lot of good, sir. Your color's back. You look so much more relaxed.

ARNOLD (*Tense*) I am.

Short pause.

HAMILTON (*To say something*) You put in late hours. This was supposed to be an easy assignment.

ARNOLD The general's coming. I wanted everything ready for him.

PEGGY And is everything ready?

ARNOLD Yes. I think so. I've done what I could. (*Cannon fire has stopped.*) They've stopped. (*Explaining*) A British frigate came a little too close.

HAMILTON I heard.

ARNOLD Must be out of range by now. And on its way.

PEGGY Colonel Hamilton's been telling me all the gossip from Philadelphia.

ARNOLD You've been there?

HAMILTON Passed through.

PEGGY The new commander's already in trouble.

ARNOLD No doubt a crook—like me. (*Beat. He reaches for the bottle and pours into Hamilton's glass; then into his own.*) Tell me something—why take it?

HAMILTON (*Confused*) I don't understand. Take what?

ARNOLD Why does *he* take it? General Washington. The crap. The lies. They'd like to kill him you know.

HAMILTON I don't think that's true—

ARNOLD (*Over this*) They'd like him to fall off his goddamn horse and break his neck. How's that?

HAMILTON That may be true for some.

ARNOLD And he knows this. (*He shakes his head and drinks.*) But then the *men* love him. He sees this. My men do. They're so excited about him arriving. Paying us the honor.

HAMILTON He's come to pay honor to you. What happened in Morristown—

ARNOLD I forget everything. A soldier has to have a short memory, Colonel. If he didn't, after being in one battle, he'd never go into another. You haven't been in a battle yet, you haven't killed yet, have you?

HAMILTON No.

ARNOLD Wait. (*He drinks.*) All is forgotten. (*Short pause*) Loved, he is. The way they speak of him. To them, a god. We know better of course. (*He winks at Hamilton, who doesn't smile.*) Oh come on—smile. You're not betraying the man by smiling. We know his faults. (*Beat*) But they love him. The men. (*He drinks.*)

HAMILTON   Like they love you.

Arnold is taken aback by this.

I better go to bed. (*He starts to go.*)

ARNOLD   Don't get me wrong. I love the general too. He's great. He's very very great.

PEGGY   I'll show you to your room.

HAMILTON   I think I can find—

PEGGY (*Over this*)   Please. I'll take the light. (*She picks up the lantern.*)

HAMILTON (*To Arnold*)   Motherhood becomes her.

PEGGY   That is a great lie, Colonel. Motherhood becomes no one. I count the days until I've shed my burden.

They go.

HANNAH   I'll clean up. (*She picks up glasses, the bottle.*) The general will be here in the morning. That is exciting. You look tired. Another drink?

Arnold nods. She pours. He drinks it all in one swallow. He stands, pushing back the chair. He sighs, exhausted; air just comes out of him, deflating him. He steadies himself as he begins to feel the drinks.

ARNOLD   Tell Peggy—I went to bed.

He goes off. After a moment the ORDERLY enters. The room is nearly dark.

ORDERLY   Is the general here?

HANNAH   He went to bed.

ORDERLY (*Hesitates, then:*)   Could you tell him, we never found Mr. Anderson.

HANNAH (*Repeating*)   You never found Mr. Anderson.

ORDERLY   Yes.

HANNAH   I'll tell him. Good night.

ORDERLY   Good night.

He goes. Peggy hurries across the room on her way to the bedroom.

HANNAH   The orderly just said—

PEGGY   Sh—sh! We need to get to sleep. (*She rubs her face.*) Tomorrow's an important day.

She goes. Hannah takes the glasses and bottle off to the kitchen.

SCENE TEN

The same. Morning. A cock crows in the distance.
      Arnold hurries in putting on his coat. Peggy, in her nightclothes and robe, runs in behind him. Hannah is alone at the table.

ARNOLD (*Shouting*)   Damn it, why wasn't I woken up? (*He goes to the door and screams to an Orderly.*) Tell His Excellency I'll be right there! I should be with him! (*He turns to Hannah.*) The general's arrived.

HANNAH   I know.

ARNOLD (*Over this, not listening*)   He's touring my forts! I look out my goddamn window and he's out there! Wake up Colonel Hamilton.

HANNAH   He's awake. And gone.

This stops Arnold and Peggy.

   He's with His Excellency.

Beat.

ARNOLD Why wasn't I woken?

HANNAH The lieutenant said not to.

ARNOLD What lieutenant?

HANNAH The one who came to get the colonel.

ARNOLD (*Confused, he looks at Peggy, then screams.*) Orderly!
Orderly!

An Orderly hurries in.

He's arrived and no one told me. The general's out there
inspecting the fortifications without me. Why would he do
that?

The Orderly doesn't know.

(*Calmer*) Mr. Anderson, you got him back safely to his ship,
did you not?

The Orderly looks at Hannah.

HANNAH (*Trying to help*) No, they—

ORDERLY We never found him, sir.

ARNOLD You never found him? You never found—Mr.
Anderson?

ORDERLY No—

ARNOLD Jesus Christ! (*He screams.*) They never found him!

HANNAH I was supposed to tell you, but Peggy said—

ARNOLD Be quiet. (*He sighs, tries to think what to do, takes
Peggy's hand.*) It'll be all right. It'll be all right.

ORDERLY Sir? A Mr. Anderson, it's being said this morning, has been captured in the village.

ARNOLD Captured? Why?

ORDERLY He's being held as a spy, sir. A British spy.

Peggy groans and nearly faints. Arnold grabs her.

ARNOLD (*To the others*) Help her to a seat. Get her to a seat!

HANNAH (*Over this*) What's—? I don't understand—?

A cannon is fired, off.

ARNOLD That's the salute for His Excellency. He's arriving. (*To Orderly*) Tell him I'll be there—momentarily. Go! Go greet His Excellency!

The Orderly, confused, hurries off.

PEGGY (*Nearly in shock*) Benedict, what's happened? I don't understand. (*She tries to reach out to him; he is lost in thought.*)

ARNOLD (*Half laughing*) Anderson. He was drunk.

PEGGY Drunk? You didn't say—

ARNOLD (*Over this*) The son of a bitch! They moored too close! I gave it to them. They had it in their hands.

PEGGY I haven't packed anything. I didn't dare.

HANNAH What's—? I don't understand!

ARNOLD (*Over this*) They could have captured Washington!

HANNAH (*Grabbing at Arnold*) Brother!

He pushes her away.

ARNOLD (*To Peggy*) Tell her.

159

Arnold moves away.

PEGGY We have—changed sides, Hannah. In this war. We now support the British.

HANNAH The British?

PEGGY (*Over this*) It was the right thing to do! We had no choice. Your brother had suffered enough humiliation.

ARNOLD (*Turning back to them*) That wasn't the reason—I wished to support—!

PEGGY (*She tries to hold him.*) I know! I know!

HANNAH (*Over this*) I know nothing of this! Why wasn't I told anything about this?

Gunshots off. Beat.

PEGGY What's . . . ?

ARNOLD The final salutes. He's here. (*Beat. To himself*) Dear God, how did this happen? (*To Peggy*) He knows. That's why they didn't send for me. They've been—looking around, to see what I've done.

PEGGY Then Andre's talked?

HANNAH Who's Andre?

ARNOLD (*Over this*) Or they found the maps. I gave him maps.

PEGGY (*Over the end of this*) You gave maps to a drunk! You stupid man!

ARNOLD He was your friend, not mine! (*He pushes Peggy away and immediately regrets it.*)

PEGGY They'll hang us.

160

HANNAH (*Cries out*) Nooooo!

More gunshots off.

ARNOLD My men know nothing. They wouldn't have been told. The British frigate's still in Haverstraw Bay. My men can row me there.

PEGGY You mean us.

Arnold just looks at her.

You're not leaving me behind. I can't stay behind!

ARNOLD It's—the safest thing. If I'm caught . . . You—don't know anything, Peggy. You—don't—know—anything.

PEGGY Don't leave me. Don't leave me. They'll kill me!

ARNOLD (*Over this*) It's the right thing! Think of the child!

Peggy grabs him and starts hitting him, shouting, "No!"

(*To Hannah*) Take her! Take her! (*To Peggy*) They will not hurt you! (*He pushes her into Hannah's arms.*)

HANNAH What about me?

ARNOLD (*Ignoring her*) I'll go across the porch. They're out front now.

PEGGY (*Being held by Hannah*) You bastard! I hate you! I hate you!

She breaks free of Hannah and attacks Arnold. Their embrace quickly turns into a hug. He holds her against his chest. She cries.

ARNOLD (*Holding her*) I'll send for you. It'll be fine. I cannot live without you. Please, Peggy.

A knock at the door.

Please, Hannah, take her. Hannah.

161

Hannah gently pulls Peggy off Arnold. And with only a quick glance back, he hurries off. Pause.
  Another knock on the door.
  Peggy slowly calms down. She takes long deep breaths.

PEGGY (*Finally, to Hannah, quietly*)   Answer it. Answer it, or they'll be suspicious.

Hannah goes and answers the door. She returns with Colonel Hamilton.
  Peggy suddenly sits up, smiles—she begins her "performance."

Colonel Hamilton. I hear you were up quite early. I hope the bed was satisfactory.

HAMILTON   It was fine, ma'am.

PEGGY   But soldiers never sleep, do they? I should know that by now. (*She smiles.*)

HAMILTON   Is your husband here? The general's anxious to speak with him.

PEGGY   My husband? He's—(*She shrugs. Then to Hannah*) Is he in his study? Hannah, see if he's in his study.

Hannah hesitates.

Hannah, please. The colonel's waiting.

Hannah goes off. Hamilton, anxious, sighs.

HAMILTON   You are sure he is in the house?

PEGGY   Is something the matter, Colonel?

He turns and looks at her.

Would you like some coffee—?

HAMILTON   Your husband has been defamed, Mrs. Arnold.

PEGGY   Who by, this time? (*She smiles.*) I've had nothing to eat myself—

HAMILTON (*Interrupting*)   Papers, plotting an assault from inside your husband's command, have been uncovered, ma'am. As well as a spy.

PEGGY   A spy? A real spy? How interesting for you.

HAMILTON   We've yet to speak with him ourselves. We've asked him to be brought here. I thought your husband should question him. Would you mind if I went upstairs to look?

PEGGY   Of course not.

Hannah returns.

HANNAH   He's not in his study.

This stops Hamilton, who is getting more and more concerned.

PEGGY   An assault from inside. I don't think I understand.

HAMILTON   Treason, Mrs. Arnold. Are you positive he didn't leave the house?

PEGGY   Where would he be going? He is expecting the general. (*She turns to Hannah.*) Did you look in our bedroom?

A Soldier bursts in.

SOLDIER   General Arnold's just been spotted in a bateau. Headed for the British frigate.

HAMILTON (*Suddenly turns*)   Stop him!

SOLDIER I believe he's too far, sir.

Beat.

HAMILTON Let the general know.

SOLDIER The general was one of those who spotted him, sir.

Short pause. Hamilton is in shock. Peggy watches him closely, then he suddenly turns on her.

HAMILTON (*Screaming*) You lied to me! You knew where he was!

PEGGY (*Frightened*) I knew nothing! What are you talking about? Hannah!

HAMILTON (*Over this*) God damn him! I believed him!

HANNAH (*Over this*) Leave her alone!

PEGGY (*Over this, begins to cry*) I knew nothing, I tell you! I promise to God! God help me, I swear!

The Soldier has gone to Hamilton to hold him back, shouting, "Sir! Sir!" Hamilton stops shouting, steps back.
Peggy collapses onto the ground and screams in pain. Hannah tries to comfort her. Between her screams, she whimpers, "I'm innocent," over and over again.

HAMILTON (*To Soldier*) Double the guard for His Excellency. His life could be in danger.

Peggy suddenly lunges toward Hamilton, pulls his sword out of his belt and attempts to slit her throat. Hannah screams, grabs the sword, cutting her hand. Hamilton pulls her away as the Soldier takes the sword. Peggy lies on the floor, trying to catch her breath, blood on her neck.

Get her to bed.

HANNAH She should see a doctor—

HAMILTON   Get her out of here!

Hannah helps Peggy up. They go out, though Peggy continues to wail and scream.

(*To himself*) I hope to God she hangs.

WASHINGTON (*Just off*)   I thought we didn't believe in God.

Hamilton turns and Washington enters from the hallway. Pause.

She didn't know anything. Listen to her. That is the sound of a broken heart.

A scream, off.

Such a man does not deserve a woman like that. And now she has to have his child. There is no justice.

HAMILTON   We should leave, sir.

Washington nods and sits.

WASHINGTON   Why did he do it, Alexander? Why? (*Beat*) His enemies are—nothing. Maggots. Compared to what he's fought. It is incomprehensible. (*He is lost in thought. Then:*) They were arriving with our—spy. Have him brought in, Colonel.

Hamilton turns to leave.

(*Stopping him*) I thought at least I was a good judge of people.

HAMILTON   General—

WASHINGTON (*Over him*)   I shall never see him again. Shall I? Or even speak his name.

Washington, in the chair, closes his eyes. Hamilton hesitates, then hurries off.

Hannah enters, on her way through the room to the kitchen.
Washington opens his eyes.

(*To Hannah*) For the life of me, I can't recall a single prayer.

HANNAH I'm getting her some water.

WASHINGTON You must know a prayer. Get me started.

Hannah hesitates, then nervously hurries out. Washington sighs.
    Andre is brought in by a Soldier and Hamilton. Andre's face is completely bloodied and his clothes torn.
    Washington does not look at him.

ANDRE Your Excellency. I wish to surrender to you.

Beat.

WASHINGTON (*His mind elsewhere; not looking at Andre*) To me?

ANDRE As an officer, sir.

WASHINGTON (*Rubbing his eyes*) You're a spy. Look at you.

Washington glances at Andre, but his mind is preoccupied for the rest of the scene.

ANDRE (*Over this*) I'm a major in the British army. Please.

WASHINGTON (*Calmly*) Hang him.

ANDRE (*Stunned*) I'm an officer in the British—!

WASHINGTON Hang him.

ANDRE I'm an officer, you can't—!

HAMILTON Sir, there should be a hearing.

Short pause. Washington remains completely distracted.

WASHINGTON   First have the hearing, then hang him. Get him out of here.

Hamilton and the Soldier drag Andre out. He struggles and yells: "You can't hang me! I'm a soldier, damn it!" etc.
  Alone, Washington stands and slowly follows them out, as Hannah enters with a pitcher of water and hurries across the stage.
  Upstairs, Peggy screams.

SCENE ELEVEN

New York City.
  Sir Henry Clinton's office. Table and chairs. MRS. HENRY CLINTON, a woman in her fifties, sits to one side and sews.
  Arnold is shown in by Kemble, who then leaves. After a moment, Sir Henry enters, all smiles.

SIR HENRY   General Arnold, it is an honor. And a pleasure.

They shake hands.

Please, sit down. May I get you something to drink?

ARNOLD   No, thank you.

Arnold sits. Pause. Sir Henry looks at Arnold and smiles.

SIR HENRY (*Finally*)   Pity about what happened. It was such an exciting prospect.

ARNOLD   I did my best. If *The Vulture* had not anchored so close to shore, then my men wouldn't have fired and—

SIR HENRY   I understand. Of course. (*Beat*) Our mistake. (*Beat*) We dumb English.

ARNOLD   I didn't say—

SIR HENRY You Americans are so much more professional at war than we are.

Short pause. He looks to his wife, who is impassive, then back to Arnold.

(*Explaining*) My wife.

ARNOLD How do you do?

She says nothing, just nods and sews.

SIR HENRY (*Sighs, then:*) I haven't slept since . . . (*He gestures to Arnold—"Since your incident," he means.*) They've put you up appropriately, I assume.

ARNOLD I'm comfortable.

SIR HENRY You feel that a man of your stature is being treated fairly?

ARNOLD I'm comfortable.

SIR HENRY I wouldn't want to hear you complain.

ARNOLD I'm not. I haven't.

SIR HENRY (*Suddenly changing the topic*) How well did you know Major Andre?

ARNOLD I only met—

SIR HENRY (*Over this*) I know you'd only met the once, but—how much did you know about him? About the sort of man he is? (*Beat*) His profound sense of dignity. His manners. His grace. He's a poet, you know. Heroic, is how I've come to see him. When I close my eyes and see him.

Mrs. Clinton turns for an instant to Sir Henry, then back to her sewing.

168

They've no right to murder such a man. He's a soldier, for one. An officer. I'll fucking murder twenty rebels if they do.

ARNOLD   Perhaps it's just a threat. They haven't killed him yet. (*Beat*) I regret what happened. But again, had *The Vulture* anchored farther—

SIR HENRY   I'm pleased you agree with me—about John Andre. A fine . . . Look what a Mr. Hamilton has sent. (*He holds up a letter.*) I gather he works for General Washington.

ARNOLD   He does.

SIR HENRY   I gather he writes without the approval of—"His Excellency." He offers to release the major.

ARNOLD   Thank God.

SIR HENRY   In exchange for you.

Pause. Arnold just looks at Sir Henry.

I could never agree to such a trade, of course. How would it look—to return you . . . Who would ever defect again? That's true, isn't it?

There is no response.

And I cannot force you to do what is right.

ARNOLD   Which is?

SIR HENRY   I can't say I've admired you, sir.

ARNOLD   I don't understand.

SIR HENRY   To betray one's cause. Even a wrong and ghastly cause as the rebels' is. But you're a soldier, man! Where's your sense of honor, I ask myself. But then I'm not

American, and I would be the first to say I don't begin to understand you Americans. (*Beat*) What you value.

ARNOLD   I've betrayed nothing—that has not already betrayed itself.

SIR HENRY   Is that right? Oh, I see. And so we do what we wish to do. Our consciences, is it? (*He smiles, then suddenly turns on him.*) And John Andre, a man I—

Mrs Clinton turns to hear this.

—admire, will be hanged because of you! Live with that!

ARNOLD (*Incredulous*)   Do you wish me to trade myself?

Short pause. No response.

You do, don't you? I do not believe this. I would think, in just pragmatic terms, my changing allegiances would be of considerable—

SIR HENRY   I doubt it. I doubt if it matters. But if that is all which stands in your way of doing a very noble act—

ARNOLD   They will kill me!

SIR HENRY   Yes. (*Beat*) But you'd die comforted by the knowledge that you'd died nobly—having saved a good soul and a great man by your death. Think about it. It is worth thinking about.

ARNOLD   I don't need to hear this—!

SIR HENRY (*Shouts*)   Think about it, I said! And you'd better do just that, because I am the only hope you have now— you have no country, no home, no friends, no family; all you've got is me! (*Pause*) Nobility, by the way, cannot be discussed in "pragmatic terms." At least I wouldn't know how. But perhaps you people have never understood that. You are so crude.

ARNOLD (*Blurting out*) Major Andre promised me money—

SIR HENRY Did he? Well go and ask him about it! Sir, this may be America, but in this office at least it is still the king's country and here the world is not only about business and money. There is something greater. Something you in this godforsaken piece of earth can't seem to understand! A decency! Virtue! And yes, honor! (*Beat*) In my two years here, sir, I have searched with great interest to discover what you Americans in fact believe in. Besides of course the freedom to cheat each other. I look in vain. Yours is a hollow race. Which, with each day—each new dawn, each new . . . (*He nods to Arnold.*) acquaintance, only disgusts me more. (*Short pause*) He is a beautiful man. Andre.

Mrs. Clinton puts down her sewing and listens to this.

Like a god.

ARNOLD He was drunk when we met—

SIR HENRY I very much doubt that. A good *English* lad— worth, one would think, slightly more than a horde of your kind. That's my personal belief. My moral belief. (*Beat*) For what it's worth. (*He smiles to Arnold.*) What do you have to live for, General Arnold? You've failed even us. You're despised—even by us. You think my soldiers will have anything but contempt for someone like you? (*He gestures to him.*) What is there to respect? So what is left? Sooner or later, you too will come to this conclusion. Why not sooner—and to save a life? (*Short pause*) The rebels have agreed to allow your wife—Peggy?—to join you here. (*Beat*)

She has refused. (*He hands Arnold Peggy's letter.*) She's chosen, she writes, to return to her family in Philadelphia, where she intends to seek an annulment of her marriage to the greatest scoundrel her young country has ever known. I don't think she's joking.

Arnold looks at the letter.

She hates you . . . The list grows and grows. Trade yourself, damn it! Die with dignity, not in some back room! Save a good man!

Major Kemble returns, his face now pale. He starts to speak, but can't.

(*Impatient*) What? What?

KEMBLE (*Holding a paper in his hand*) Major Andre—has been hanged. (*He hands Sir Henry the paper. Pause*) I suggest we hang three prisoners this hour—our response. That we fucking cut off their heads and stick pikes through their skulls. (*Beat*) Do I have your permission, sir?

Beat. Clinton, in a daze, nods.

It is said he died with honor. (*Beat*) That rarely has a man faced death with such calm. Even rebel officers—(*He nods toward the paper.*)—were seen to weep. His one regret, which he spoke just before his death, was that he was to be hanged, not shot, as is more appropriate for a gentleman. (*Beat*) He died—like an Englishman.

Sir Henry holds his head in his hands. Kemble turns to Arnold.

Why don't you go.

Arnold hesitates, then:

172

ARNOLD   Sir Henry, I wish to know if you intend to honor the financial arrangement agreed to by Major Andre. (*Beat*) I have nothing. I was promised ten thousand pounds.

Sir Henry looks up at Arnold.

SIR HENRY   Get this scum out of my office! Get him out!

Sir Henry goes to draw his sword. Kemble holds him back. Sir Henry suddenly begins to moan and howl in great pain.
   Mrs. Clinton stands, sets down her sewing. Kemble tries to comfort Sir Henry.

MRS. CLINTON (*To Kemble*)   Take him to his bedroom. He should lie down.

Kemble helps Sir Henry off. He continues to moan.

(*To Arnold*) My husband—liked Major Andre very much. That must be clear. (*Beat*) He spent so much time with him. He is—was—a charming man. A pleasure to be with. So I'm told. My husband seemed always to be thinking about him. He would say things—and I would know this. That he was thinking of John. (*Beat*) I was even a little jealous.

Sir Henry moans, off.

I'll go and comfort him now. (*She nods to Arnold and leaves.*)

Arnold hesitates. Sir Henry howls, "John!" off; then Arnold leaves the office.

New York City. Sitting room of Arnold's temporary residence. Table, chairs. Hannah sits with a MR. ROBINSON, *a twenty-year-old American loyalist; they are just finishing tea.*

HANNAH (*In the middle of a story*) I hadn't known this, but my brother had already told this man, two or three times, that he'd best stay away from me.

ROBINSON (*Very interested*) This was the Frenchman.

HANNAH Yes. Now I knew that General Arnold hated French people.

ROBINSON Who doesn't? The other day I heard a joke about the French; it was very funny. Very true. I wish I could remember it.

HANNAH (*As an afterthought*) And he loved the English.

ROBINSON (*As if the most obvious thing in the world*) Of course!

HANNAH But my Frenchman was so handsome!

She and Robinson laugh at this.

And I was—I wasn't always old.

Robinson starts to offer a compliment.

Don't say a word. I'm not asking for lies.

ROBINSON It was not a lie I was about to speak.

She looks at him, smiles.

HANNAH But—it was our money the Frenchman was after. My brother told me this later. We had a lot of property. We were society—in New Haven.

Robinson nods.

ROBINSON   That means something, I know.

HANNAH   So on one of my Frenchman's visits to me,
Benedict arrives with a friend at the front door, asks his
friend to knock and he, my brother, goes out back and
hides in the bushes—

Arnold enters. Robinson immediately stands and smiles.

ROBINSON   Sir, it is an honor.

*He holds out his hand to shake; Arnold takes it. He turns to
Hannah.*

HANNAH   Mr. Robinson. He has an uncle with a house—
where is it in London?

ROBINSON   The Brompton Road.

HANNAH   That's supposed to be a very nice area. Lots of
Americans live there. There's still a little tea—

*Arnold shakes his head, then sits. Robinson sits back down, not
knowing what to say.*

Let me just finish my story. So the general is out back in
the bushes. My suitor—(*To Arnold*) the French boy—
hearing someone coming in the front door, suddenly throws
open a window and jumps out—into the arms of—him.
And then you whipped him, right? (*Beat*) He's always
protected me. (*She takes Arnold's hand. Short awkward pause*)

ROBINSON   (*Finally, to Arnold*)   We admired very much what
you attempted to achieve, General. It's a pleasure to have a
man like yourself on our side.

Arnold looks at Robinson, who sips his tea.

HANNAH   Mr. Robinson comes from—how far north of
Albany is that?

ROBINSON (*To Arnold*) You probably know the estate. It's quite a sizeable tract—

ARNOLD (*Over this*) *That* Robinson, yes. And there was a beautiful manse—

ROBINSON (*Over this*) I was born in that house!

ARNOLD Were you? It's gone now—

ROBINSON I've been told that—

ARNOLD I burned it down. (*Beat*) Not me personally. On my orders. While retreating from Quebec. Quite the manse. It was in the way. But now, as you say, we're on the same side. (*Arnold stands and holds out his hand.*) Perhaps we'll meet someday on the Brompton Road, Mr. Robinson.

Robinson hesitates, then realizes he is being told the tea is over. He stands and shakes hands.

HANNAH Mr. Robinson, it was a pleasure. At last—some intelligent conversation! (*She smiles.*)

ROBINSON Thank you—for the tea. I should go. I'm expected . . . General—God save the king. I'll show myself out. (*He goes.*)

HANNAH I am trying to make friends.

Arnold has looked at his pocket watch.

She's late. Does that surprise you?

There is no response.

There's another account in this morning's paper from Philadelphia.

ARNOLD I've read enough accounts—

HANNAH It appears not only did she denounce you publicly, she walked in the procession—

ARNOLD (*Yells over this*) I don't want to know!

HANNAH (*Newspaper in hand*) This isn't love!

ARNOLD She's a child.

HANNAH No she isn't.

ARNOLD She did what she had to—to survive. They made her. She made a mistake.

HANNAH Is that why she's coming here—to survive? Is that enough for you?

She has hurt him. Short pause.

I just don't want you hurt, that is all. You make your bed, you lie in it, you don't keep trying to wriggle out. That's what I can't abide.

ARNOLD I know what you can't abide, Hannah! Now be quiet!

The doorbell rings, off.

Beat.

It rings again.

HANNAH I'll go. (*She starts, then turns back.*) I have stood with you, brother. I never—questioned. (*Beat*) That is what love is. I'll get the door. (*She goes.*)

Off, the sound of a baby crying. Arnold sits and waits.
After a moment, Peggy, no longer pregnant, enters, taking off her hat. They look at each other. The baby cries, off.

ARNOLD Hannah doesn't know babies. Maybe you should . . .

PEGGY   She'll do fine.

Beat.

ARNOLD (*Referring to the baby*)   Is that—ours?

She nods.

How was the journey? Would you like to sit down?

She shakes her head.

(*He gestures to the room.*) It's temporary until . . . I tried to make it as comfortable as possible. I hope you approve, Peggy. (*Pause*) I am very sorry you were not allowed to remain in Philadelphia.

She shrugs.

PEGGY (*As if explaining.*)   The wife of Benedict Arnold . . . Even the innocent wife. Or so most believed—

He reaches for her hand.

ARNOLD   Sit down, sit down.

The baby stops crying.

I want to see him.

PEGGY   Yes. (*She sits.*)

ARNOLD   I can try to find you a different house to stay in, should you not wish—should you wish to be alone.

PEGGY (*Not answering*)   It's comfortable. Your sister's done an admirable job.

Short pause.

ARNOLD   You look splendid.

PEGGY (*Laughs*)   No, I don't. (*She looks into his face.*) You are the most hated man—ever. I don't understand. (*She looks away.*) I was forced to watch them drag a likeness—

ARNOLD (*Trying to stop her*)   I read about—

PEGGY (*Over this*)   —a likeness of you, through the streets, dragged by a rope around its neck. The screams of people. What they said. (*She shakes her head.*) I attacked you. Someone put a club in my hand, so I hit. I marched with them. Someone called out, "spit on him!" (*Beat*) So I spat— on you. (*Beat*) I thought then they'd let me stay. (*Beat*) I'm very sorry.

He looks at her.

ARNOLD   I make no judgment. How can I?

PEGGY   They burned you—a face on each side of a head. Two faces?

He nods that he understands.

With horns. My family's all denounced you. And when we were told I'd have to leave, what could they do? They begged. (*She shrugs.*)

ARNOLD   And why do they think I did it?

PEGGY   Who?

ARNOLD (*Shrugs*)   Your family—

PEGGY (*Quickly*)   For money.

He closes his eyes.

That's the reason everybody gives. You were paid ten thousand pounds by—

ARNOLD I haven't gotten it; I've asked—

PEGGY Then you did want money?

ARNOLD For a reimbursement—my pay—what I'd—I was owed—(*He looks at her.*) Forget it. I made a deal with Andre. Nothing's in writing.

PEGGY For some reason, he's become a hero, Andre. They say he died so—well. I've tried to explain to my sisters that he's an actor—

ARNOLD (*Realizing*) Of course! That's why—

PEGGY But, now he's a hero. It makes no sense. Nothing does. I hate this country. May it rot in hell. May it sink to the bottom of the ocean. I felt so used! Who the hell do they think they are? I don't know what they see that's so *good*! (*She almost cries, but stops herself.*) The things people are made to do. I love my father. He is my father. That's his crime. Now they must humiliate him. (*Beat*) I'd like to stay here with my husband.

He looks at her.

Until we sail together. London will be so grand, Benedict! I see it already. The theatres, the shops. I've seen etchings— you've already been—

ARNOLD I was a boy!

PEGGY (*Continuing*) And I think there can't be anyplace better. I think we're lucky. That's what I told my sister. You'll be respected. After what you've done. Like you must be respected here by the British. Giving you this house. And ten thousand pounds!

He watches her.

And then we'll win the war and come back, and then we'll see who has a carriage. We'll see who's made to spit on whose husband! (*She starts to weep.*) Oh Benedict.

He goes and hugs her.

I'm so frightened. I want to go home.

Pause as they hug.

ARNOLD   Peggy? One of the charges against me? (*He tries to get her attention.*) That the committee made against me? They said I profited by letting a ship—giving it a pass. (*Beat*) I did . . . profit. I did own a share.

She looks at him.

I did that.

Short pause.

PEGGY (*Incredulous*)   So what? (*Then on to a new subject*) God knows what I'll miss. What do you think you'll miss?

He shrugs.

ARNOLD   There's probably—some smell? That a country has, that you don't even notice while you're there but you notice it when it's gone. (*Beat*) Probably some—fertile smell. I don't know. (*He takes deep breaths, trying to calm himself.*) We've been offered passage—next week.

Suddenly, off, the baby begins to cry again. They listen.

I don't even know his name. It *is* a—?

She nods. Beat.

PEGGY (*Then:*)   George.

He looks at her.

After the king.

This makes him suddenly laugh, and the laugh is enough to break him and he begins to sob.
    The baby cries, off.
    Peggy watches her husband. Then she stands and helps him up.

PEGGY Come on. He needs you to hold him. And comfort him.

They go off.

The baby continues to cry.

SCENE THIRTEEN

Twenty-one years later. Hallway outside the chamber of the House of Representatives. A gavel is being pounded.

Hamilton stands with one or two REPRESENTATIVES *in the doorway.*

HAMILTON What's this about?

Others shrug and turn to listen as a VOICE *shouts over the chamber noise.*

VOICE Mr. Speaker! Mr. Speaker!

More pounding.

    Mr. Speaker! May I have the floor please?!

The noise dips, then:

    Thank you. Gentlemen, I have an announcement. It is my pleasure to report to this body—the death in London of Benedict Arnold.

A stirring is heard.

The most heinous man America has known—is dead at last!

Cheers.

It is reported that our embassy received a request from the family to bring the body back here.

Shouts of "NO," etc.

That request was quickly denied!

Cheers. The Representatives go into the chamber, leaving Hamilton alone onstage, listening.

And relish the news that he died in penury and squalor, hated and shunned by all decent men of all nations. A just reward, is it not?

Beat.

May his be a lesson for all traitors. That God watches over us. He watches over America. With this just death, we all may breathe easier and with the knowledge that America is safer, one enemy is no more.

Beat.

How comforting it is, in times like our own, when daily the world looms diffuse and vague, to be reminded of the simple unassailable truth: There is right and wrong. There is good and evil. And there is justice. God bless America!

The entire chamber shouts out: "God bless America!"

Hamilton closes the door.

Silence. He slowly walks off.

End of play.